MARK FRENCH, JAY POSICK & RYAN SHEEHY

PRINCIPALS IN ACTION

REDEFINING THE ROLE

AF207358

Published by EduGladiators LLC (www.edugladiators.com)

Book Design & Production: EduGladiators LLC

Paperback ISBN: 978-1-7340514-2-1

ebook ISBN: 978-1-7340514-3-8

PRAISE FOR PRINCIPALS IN ACTION

The principalship is an isolating position. We often see building leaders who burn out because the day to day stress has the tendency to take the joy out of the job. *Principals in Action* helps you find that joy through easy to do activities that help keep your focus on student and staff well being. From good news calls of the day to growing your PLN to developing a vision for the building, Principals in Action will help new and veteran leaders grow substantially!

- Joe Sanfelippo
Fall Creek Superintendent, author, and speaker #GoCrickets

Principals in Action is more than another school leadership book. It is a lasting testament for the purpose and passion of the principal gig all written by three sincere servant leaders. Mark French, Jay Posick and Ryan Sheehy bring their wisdom, expertise and learning a book that calls you to action. I sure wish that I had this book back when I was in "principal school." This power trio of author-principals takes the lessons they have shared at various conferences and Twitter chats and compiled into the book you are holding. Along the way, you will meet other leaders who are doing the work in service of schools. Mark, Jay and Ryan empower and inspire. This book is a true gift for school leadership and you will be inspired to action for years to come after reading Principals in Action.

- Sean Gaillard
Principal and Author of *The Pepper Effect*

This is the book I've been waiting for! *Principals in Action* is a practical book that will inspire school leaders and remind them of their 'why.' Principals don't build school culture in their office; they build it in the hallways, in the classrooms, in the cafeteria, and in the carpool line. These authors get it! Mark French, Jay Posick, and Ryan Sheehy understand the value of relationships and the power of engaging with everyone in the building. This is a book written by principals and for principals.

- Danny Steele
Educator, Author, and Speaker

More than a book, this is a very accessible guide school leaders can use to grow. French, Posick, and Sheehy share practitioner-friendly stories that challenge and inspire. There's so much to love in these pages, but what I appreciate most is knowing this book represents the power of us...and in that simple truth the heart of servant leadership beats strong.

- Brad Gustafson
Award-Winning Principal and Author

Jay, Ryan, and Mark have crafted a book that encapsulates the *Principals in Action* movement perfectly. They outline a blueprint to inspiring and connected leadership that will transform your learning community. I am a proud Principal in Action and I highly recommend this book to all leaders who are looking to raise their leadership to another level. Not only will you walk away with dozens of ideas, you will finish this book feeling blessed with three new friends and mentors.

- Allyson Apsey
Elementary Principal, Author of *Through the Lens of Serendipity*

Being a principal can be a lonely position, but only if you let it. Mark, Jay and Ryan are just a few of the principals across the world with a connected Professional Learning Network that YOU can connect with to learn and grow with. *Principals in Action* is packed with their stories, inspiration, and great ideas to help you be a Principal in Action.

- Jessica Johnson
Principal, Author, and Speaker

Being a principal can be the most satisfying job, but also a lonely one. *Principals in Action* is a resource that will make any school leader feel as if they have their tribe at their fingertips. Bringing the fun into the role with energizing challenges and stories, the book will help principals engage in activities that are meaningful and centered around stakeholders. From good news calls to having fun with kids, gone are the days of isolation for school leaders. Get ready to be inspired and change the way you lead!"

- Lynmara Colón
Director, Author, and Speaker

The role of a campus principal has evolved beyond measure. Having served as a principal, or a lead learner as I prefer to be called, for six years, I can truly acknowledge that being a principal is not the same as being a *Principal in Action*. Becoming a Principal in Action changed the trajectory of my leadership path. The mantra speaks for itself - Get Out of the Office - for that is truly where the magic happens.

- Onica L. Mayers
Director, Human Resources & Forever Lead Learner

The modern day school principal position brings many unique challenges that are not aligned to leadership preparation programs. #PrincipalsInAction provides a road map to meet these challenges by increasing your positive engagement with staff and students. Jay, Mark, and Ryan do a great job giving insight and reflection into how these have been implemented in real schools, not just as a theory. New or experienced principals would really benefit from these leadership innovations. Read today!

- Andy Jacks
National Distinguished Principal from Virgina

Principals In Action was for me what *Kids Deserve It* was for so many teachers...a game changer. Through Jay, Mark and Ryan's experiences, we learn valuable ideas and takeaways that we can implement in our schools tomorrow. It also challenges you to be engaged and break down the walls of your school to have a bigger impact. I especially enjoy that every chapter pushes us to take our passion for educational leadership and turn it into a win for students, staff and parents. If you don't know what it means to be a Principal In Action, I challenge you to read this book and watch your passion come to life for your school!

- Kelley Begley McCall
Principal of Clear Creek Elementary in Shawnee, KS

No matter how long you've been a principal, whether it be 1 month or 15 years, I guarantee you will find some golden nuggets of wisdom that you can apply tomorrow. Every chapter will get you excited to keep pushing yourself on the journey of being a Principal in Action!

- Jessica Gomez
Proud Principal of Alice Birney Elementary

I would like to thank all the students, colleagues, educators and leaders who have inspired, supported, mentored, and challenged me. T

hank you to my husband Kip who patiently listens to all my stories, has been a video wizard for my schools, and gives me great advice. To all my Principals In Action friends, thank you for your friendship.

~ Mark

This book is dedicated to every educator that is trying to change the world. Your work is meaningful and truly makes a difference in the lives of others.

I want to thank my parents Bill and Diana Sheehy for raising me into the man I am today. To my seven siblings (Nik, Kyne, Sara, Luke, Tim, Will, & Elise) for helping shape me in my younger years. To my wife, Barbara and my four children (Robert, Joshua, Julianna, & Zachary) thank you for making me want to make the world a better place for you.

Thank you to all of my Principal In Action friends for pushing my thinking and making me a better leader and a better person. This book and this movement can change education and the way it is lead and it would not have happened without every single one of you.

~ Ryan

This book is dedicated to…my parents, Joe and Liz Posick, who were my first teachers and are still my teachers to this day, who have pushed me to be better and have cheered me along the way.

My siblings, Brian and Priscilla, who have always supported my passion as an educator and, through raising their own children, have helped me look for different ways to be an impactful educator.

My daughter, Lauren, who lived with a dad who was often more focused on school than her, but still loves him anyway, and who helped me see, through her eyes, the need to be a different principal than the norm.

My wife, Jenifer, who has been by my side throughout my over 30 years in education as a teacher, coach, and administrator. She has seen the good, the bad, and everything in between and has supported me through it all. She has told me for as long as I can remember that I should write a book.

Well, I did it! I love you all and cannot thank you enough for your continued support and encouragement.

~ Jay

Contents

Forward by Adam Welcome

Introduction

Forward

Adam Welcome

"You can't go down the slide, Mr. Welcome." - 2nd grader.

"I can do whatever I want!"

The interaction I had that day with that 2nd grader at my school, and the ensuing photo that was taken and shared on social media, changed my life not only as a school Principal, but as an educator in general.

Not too long ago, I was an educator in peril.

Frustrated. Upset. Discouraged. And ready to leave the profession. I decided it was time to go 'all in' on Twitter and really build out my professional learning network so I could have a group of people to lean on, collaborate with, commiserate with and learn from on a daily basis.

Blogging had been a big part of my personal and professional life for a while as well, and the connections that came from all that writing have no doubt helped shape who I am today as an educator, but I felt something was missing. I couldn't put my finger on it but I knew inside something had to change. Something big had to happen. The time had come and I needed to figure out what it was.

One morning super early as I went for my daily run, it came to me. If I could connect every single Principal across the country we could be stronger, smarter, more efficient and better for each other and the schools where we worked. That very morning after my run I started it.

A Voxer group made up of only principals. This would be the place where we would connect, laugh, cry, teach each other and have a 24/7 lifeline to others around the country that were doing the same exact job as each other. Principals In Action was born and it took off like a missile into educational orbit.

I shared that slide photo with the world on Twitter and put out my idea to the world. "If you want to join an all principal group on Voxer, send me a message. We're going to change the world."

The group grew rapidly, I added leaders that I knew, who hadn't even messaged me they wanted to join, I decided they needed to join. We talked. People posed questions. They shared stories of success, and stories of heartbreak. After being only a few months old, the group was my go to place for all things leadership and the notifications on my phone were going besirk! And do you want to know what happened?

I was happy. I was excited about work. I felt more confident because I had my team, my people, the ones who I knew would be there for me no matter what. Ready to answer questions. Connect on a side Voxer message, and others felt the same exact way. It was therapy for us all and I couldn't remember what life as a principal was like before I had started Principals In Action.

That 2nd grade student is what really made this all come to fruition. I was a principal, the leader at my school and my goal from day one was to always be the 'un-principal' and like no other leader my teachers, students and parents had experienced. You can't be that leader or much of a leader at all if you're sitting in the office all day planning budgets, answering emails and NOT connecting with your school. And you really can't be a leader if you're not connected with your people and learning, and growing, and laughing, and changing, and remaining relevant for the people you have in your school community.

Principals In Action is alive and well to this day many years later. I urge you to join the group or start your own. Voice is a very powerful tool and it connects humans in a very profound way. So find your people, they're out there, they want to connect, they want to grow, and they want to do it with you.

Go be awesome for each other!

Introduction

The role of the principal is constantly changing. As our students change, as state requirements change, and other variables change, leaders need to change to stay effective to ensure that our students are being served. Even though the role of the principal is changing, there are some who see the principal as the stereotypical disciplinarian who sits in their office, waits for problems, and talks to students who make poor choices.

Principals In Action was started by one principal, Adam Welcome, throwing out a challenge for principals to get outside their office and ride a slide with kids. From there it has exploded. Principals are connected with each other, constantly pushing each other's daily practice. Challenges are proposed weekly, raising the bar on education leaders and the level of experience our students are receiving.

Throughout these chapters, read real-life stories from principals of all three levels, and our personal journeys as an administrator. Experience emotions that are real in our kids' lives on a daily basis.

This book will take leaders on a journey through stories

and ways that can simply enhance leadership practices and build relationships. By being out of the office and in classrooms, you will be able to see your students and staff in action more regularly and not just during the obligatory formal evaluation process. Being present for staff and students allows a principal to share the great things going on in schools, provide more meaningful support for staff, and let students know that principals are learners, too. Every leader can get out of their office and be a principal in action.

If we want "innovation" to flourish in our schools, we have to be willing to immerse ourselves in the environments where it is going to happen. If you're thinking you don't have the time, remember that your technology is mobile. You can do what I did; take your computer or tablet and work in classrooms.
~ George Couros, The Innovator's Mindset

There is so much good that can happen when principals are out of their office. We can greet students and families at student drop off, walk the hallways, especially during passing times, stop into classrooms to learn with students and staff, eat lunch with the students, participate in recess, and wish them a good rest of their day when the students leave for the day. Our hope is that this book will provide ideas, and maybe even reasons, for all school administrators to get out of their office and become a real part of the school. The view from the office is such a minuscule part of the life of the school.

GET OUT OF YOUR OFFICE and get into your school!

Principals In Action

Chapter 1

Principals Then and Now

(Jay Posick)

Allow me to set the stage for you. I was having a conversation about being a principal with some of my wife's friends. They heard about Ryan, Mark, and I writing this book so it wasn't just a random conversation or a topic I decided to drop in for small talk. After telling me I was crazy for being a middle school principal (I get that a lot), I asked them one question, "Do you remember your principal?"

Silence, except for one person who remembered their assistant principal from middle school because of the number of discussions they had with him. Otherwise, my wife's friends didn't remember seeing their principal or even their name. Honestly, that's just sad. As a principal, or an educator, we have a chance to make an impression on the people we serve.

What kind of impression do you want to make?

What kind of relationships do you want to develop with your students, staff, and families?

Now it's your turn. Think about your principal from elementary school, or middle school, or high school. Do you remember their name?

I remember one of my elementary school principals (I moved a lot before middle school), Mr. Crosby, because his name was on the middle school building I attended the following year. I also remember meeting with him in his office because I no longer was able to be the crossing guard in front of the school, but that's a different story.

My middle school principal, Mr. Offerdahl, also comes to mind not because of anything in school, but because I later worked for him at an ice cream stand in Land O' Lakes, WI. Because we attended the same church, I also remember my high school principal, Mr. Arnold.

None of these interactions really stand out to me as "knowing my principal", though. All three were good people, but I didn't really know them as principals. Recently I had an interview for a middle school principal position at a nearby school. One of the students on the interview team said this when I asked him what his current principal does, "It's a complete mystery to me."

That really struck me. As I think back about the three principals I mentioned, what they did was also a complete mystery to me. When I asked Ryan and Mark the same question, they too had a difficult time remembering their principal.

Ryan had no idea who his elementary school principal was. Middle school was easier because it was a small school, but he never saw her interact with kids. His high school principal was memorable for one reason - he would walk around yelling at kids. None of those principals left a positive lasting impression. Rather they all made Ryan want to be better and to leave his students with a long-lasting impression of what principals actually do and how much they care about their students.

Mark remembers his elementary and middle school principals' names, but can't ever recall seeing them visiting classrooms, being on the playground, hanging out in the cafeteria, or greeting students at arrival. That is not what many principals did in the 60s and 70s. The one principal Mark recalls fondly is his high school principal, Mr. Granlund. Mark does remember seeing Mr. Granlund in the hallways, at school activities, and at athletic events. Mr. Granlund took an interest in his students, got to know them, and worked on developing relationships. Mr. Granlund served as one of Mark's early role models as he worked on his elementary education degree, did his student teaching, during his first teaching position, and as he ventured into school administration.

Think back to your principals and tell me if this isn't what you remember about them.
- Spent most if not all of their day in the office.
- Made the morning or afternoon announcements.
- Had a paddle hanging proudly on their wall.

- No one wanted to go to the principal's office because it meant that you were in trouble.
- Always wore a suit and tie.
- They were gruff and grumbly and not happy.
- Usually males and mostly white males.
- When they walked through the hallways, everyone moved out of their way and stopped talking.

I'm sure there are other things to add to the list, but this is a good start. It's also a time for reflection as we think about our role as a principal and what people think about us. If someone asked one of our students, staff or families what I do as principal, I sure hope they wouldn't say, "It's a complete mystery."

Reflecting on what I do, and what the principals I am connected with do, I try to do the things that are on this list.

- I'm out of my office more than I'm in my office.
- I schedule time on my calendar to be out of my office.
- I let my secretary know where I'm going and why I'm going there in case someone is looking for me.
- Our secretary texts me if I'm needed in my office (I don't carry a walkie talkie because they are distracting when they go off in a classroom.)
- Our superintendent knows to text me, email me, or send me a message via Google hangouts if he needs me for anything.
- I'm in classrooms, hallways, the cafeteria, and the playground every day.
- I'm at the student drop off in the morning and student pick up in the afternoon.
- I wear my "jammypack" for student drop off, lunch and recess, and student pick up.

- I sit down and eat lunch with students from time to time.
- I participate in student dress up days.

There are many more things that you can add, I'm sure, but the point is that principals now should be different than principals then. Students and teachers have changed so principals should have changed, too.

What changes are you willing to make so that tomorrow, next week or next year, when someone asks one of the people you serve if they remember their principal, they can say, "Yes I do. She/he was everywhere, was always smiling, listened to me, and provided advice and support when I needed it. And her/his name is Miss/Mrs./Ms./Mr. _____."

Challenge

Look at the second list of descriptors and choose one of them to focus on over the next week or month. Share evidence by using the Twitter hashtag #PrincipalsInAction to show the descriptor you focused on.

Chapter 2

Good News Call of The Day

(Mark French)

Often people ask us what is the best advice that was ever given to me to prepare me to be a leader. The response is always the same: "Relationships, Relationships, Relationships." As the leader of building rapport in our schools, relationships are often at the forefront of this important quality. We need to work on building relationships with students, staff, families, and the community. Our stakeholders need to know who we are and what we stand for, and we need to be available to them through a variety of communication tools. It's not enough to be available only through technology. Those face to face meetings and telephone conversations are also vital to make connections.

"Hello, this is the principal calling.

In the summer of 2015, I was participating in a Twitter chat and was impressed when a teacher shared that she made a positive phone call home for one of her students every day. I thought, I have 750 students and can certainly find one student a day deserving of a positive phone call home. #GoodNewsCallOfTheDay was born.

That year (2015-2016) I created a spreadsheet and tracked my 130 different positive phone calls. Actually, I made more than 130 calls, I selected 130 different students that year. For some students, I called both parents, other family members - whoever they wanted me to call. I also took a selfie with the student and shared the photo and reason for the call on social media.

The following year (2016-2017) I continued my #GoodNewsCallOfTheDay making calls for 135 different students that year. I continued with the selfie and sharing on social media and I bought #GoodNewsCallOfTheDay wristbands to give each student for them to remember and show others. This has turned out to be a powerful practice taking less than 15 minutes each day and using an easy technology tool, the telephone. I'm now in my fourth year of making these calls and making my positive phone call home is the best part of my day.

During the 2016-2017 school year, Jay had a goal similar to mine- make one positive phone call home. He failed miserably except for one beautiful Friday in April. Jay had every teacher provide him with at least one student and made phone calls most of the day on that Friday. It was one of the highlights of the year for Jay and, more importantly, it made the kids and their families feel good.

After a summer of learning and challenges by #PrincipalsInAction, Jay renewed his goal of making a #GoodNewsCallOfTheDay, but with a little bit of a twist. He continued meeting with his grade level teams every Thursday and added an agenda item is to provide him with the name of a student to receive a #GoodNewsCallOfTheDay. Those not on grade level teams also provided him with names. If there are any "extra" names, Jay encourages the teachers to make the calls themselves as it's a great way to build positive relationships with families. An added benefit to having the staff provide names is that they can provide the reasons for the call home. Jay has continued this agenda item with grade level teams ever since.

Jay provides a pass for the students to come to the office for the call. The students do a great job setting up the call by saying, "Hi, mom or dad. I'm in Mr. Posick's office and he has something important to talk about with you." Jay takes over from there, assuring the family that their child isn't in trouble or injured, and then reads the good news from the staff to the family. Once the call is over, Jay gives the student a #GoodNewsCallOfTheDay wristband, takes a photo of the student in his office with a hashtag and sends it home to their families. One week Jay added one more twist as he asked staff to nominate a colleague for a #GoodNewsCallOfTheDay. The staff nominated a teacher, he called the husband of the teacher, and the three of them had a really good cry. The relationships fostered by sharing good news to a student or staff member's family cannot be underestimated.

When Ryan became a vice principal of a high school, he knew that he needed to do something to make sure that he wasn't only calling home for discipline issues or problems. Ryan needed to get parents and students to understand that the school cares about the positive things that are going on as well. Thinking back to the first call he made, the parents were shocked. Ryan had chosen a student that had been in trouble before, but on this day made a great decision and helped out a student who was down on their luck. As soon as Ryan caught him doing something good, he jumped at the opportunity to spread the joy.

As Ryan transitioned into becoming an elementary school principal, calling home for good things was a must. These phone calls have established positive relationships with both parents and students. Ryan now makes it a point every year before the 100th day of school, he has made 100 positive phone calls home. You can check out the Twitter hashtag #GoodNewsCallOfTheDay to see other educators making positive phone calls and smiling students. Make it a practice to share the positive and recognize the good things happening in your school.

Remember, If you're not telling your school's story, someone else will.

Challenge

Findonestudentorstaffmemberfora#GoodNewsCallOfTheDay today. Don't just limit yourself to students or teachers. Think about your office staff, custodians, paraprofessionals, cafeteria staff, school resource officers, counselors, psychologists, social workers, and bus drivers. Involve your staff in providing you names and reasons for calling home.

Chapter 3

Challenge Yourself

(Ryan Sheehy)

Every fall when school starts back up it is important to start thinking, *How do you challenge yourself?* Jay Posick, Mark French, and I are principals that have connected through being in a personal or professional learning network (PLN) called Principals In Action - a group that was started by one of the *Kids Deserve It* authors, Adam Welcome.

The Principals in Action hashtag started with a challenge by Adam to ride the slide with kids then tweet the picture using the #PrincipalsInAction hashtag. The group is now so much more than a hashtag. Using Voxer as our communication platform, we communicate on a daily basis, discussing triumphs, struggles, and the everyday occurrences of being a principal. We currently are a group of over 300 administrators that have made a goal of being out of the office and truly being a principal in action. Our group stretches from coast to coast and everywhere in between.

One of the ways we have been able to challenge each other on a daily basis is through creating challenges that everyone participates in, then tweets about using the #PrincipalsInAction hashtag. These challenges come out each week and are posted all over Twitter by using the hashtag. This past year some of the challenges included: ride a tricycle, ride the bus, serve food in the lunchroom, eat lunch with students, play on the swings, and read to students. These challenges are constantly pushing administrators out of their office and out with kids and staff.

For me, being part of this PLN during my early stages of my principalship provided me a level of encouragement, professional development, and outside thinking that I was not getting in my district. The challenges provided me an excuse to document some of the fun things I was doing outside of my office. I have shown up to principal meetings and my colleagues look at me and say, "Ryan, it always looks like you are having fun." I am and I show it off because school should be fun and the challenges had that component for me. I have enjoyed riding tricycles, slipping down slides, serving lunch in the cafeteria, and just being with kids.

We need to be the one that shows teachers, students, and parents that principals need to be with kids, not in their office. Cafeterias across the country have notoriously been known for not having super friendly people, which is an unfair stereotype because I know many amazing cafeteria workers. Here I was a 2nd year principal and the challenge was to serve lunch to students. I headed into the cafeteria like I normally do at the lunch hour. This time instead of walking around, I headed back to the kitchen. The ladies in the kitchen looked at me like I was alien when I asked if I could help serve lunch today. They told me they have never had anyone else come and help, not even the kitchen supervisors. I spent the lunch hour serving to every student that came through. It was such an enriching opportunity for myself because I got to put myself in their shoes and truly understand why things happen a certain and how I can support them better with.

For Jay, he was in his tenth year as a principal in the same building. Principals In Action provided the inspiration and support to get out of his office, interact with students and staff, and accept challenges. Jay honestly doesn't remember all of the challenges, but he does remember his favorite one - shadowing a student for a day. Jay actually shadowed two students: a 6th grader in the morning and a 7th grader in the afternoon. Lunch and recess duties were sandwiched between the two shadowing opportunities. The day was spent in classrooms learning right alongside the students. Interested students filled out a Google form and then a random number selector determined who he shadowed. Jay reflected on the day and realized the students and staff were awesome that day and it was amazing being in the classrooms with them as a student. Jay thinks the staff enjoyed him being in their classrooms far more than an observation or a walkthrough, too.

What if it is you?
Joy Wright, Middle School Principal, West Hartford, CT

With all of the awesomeness of being a principal, there are times when you will face challenges. Most often, our challenges are not our own doing. Every day, we lead through unfunded mandates, inequality issues, transportation delays, school tragedies, challenging behaviors, and budget crisis. But sometimes, the challenges we face are our own doing. What if, despite your good intentions, you failed to hit the mark and it caused factions in your staff and got in the way of effectively serving your school community? What do you do then? I faced this situation a few years ago in my second school principalship, and I learned that the best course of action for a principal in action is to respond like a learner.

I joined my second principalship at a wonderful middle school in an impressive district during a time of great educational upheaval as the state was implementing a new teacher evaluation system and moving into the second year of common core. I started at the school in early August with just a day or so of transition with the outgoing principal before I would welcome new teachers in a few weeks.

Did I mention that I also had to hire a new assistant principal and that the current one was only five months into the job? There were many things out of my control, but I hit the ground running. Once school started, I was determined to hear from my community. I set up office hours for parents and staff with the intention of getting to know them, listening to their needs, and building a community of understanding and support. Halfway through the first year, it was clear that my efforts were not working. The staff did not feel connected, and there was a concern that the new leadership team did not value all of the great work done previously. To make sure that we were working as a cohesive community, we came together during a number of professional learning times to identify our major commitments and priorities that we now call our Big Rocks. This collaborative work identified our focus areas as a staff community, and we determined that our efforts would be directed by student success, staff wellness, and community engagement.

After adopting them, publishing them and linking to everything we do, I was proud of the collaborative way we established our collective focus. I was confident that this would do "the trick" for improving staff morale. However, while we were in a better place concerning our vision, there was still a challenge, and it turned out that for a number of my staff, it was me. How does a leader respond when she is told that she is the problem? The only way an educator should, from a place of reflection and learning.

When I asked what I could do better, the answer wasn't about being a more capable instructional leader or connecting better with students or offering more resources for support. A portion of my staff felt like I needed to do a better job of connecting with them. They did not feel like I cared about them and this was getting in the way of maintaining a positive school climate. On the end of the year school climate survey, one staff member noted that he/she felt I was good at being a parent and student-principal, but that I needed to be a better teacher-principal.

Ouch! I won't lie, I was hurt, but I could not argue with the consistency of the feedback I heard from some of my staff. So, after gathering the initial feedback, and licking my wounds, I did what all great learners do, I read books about how to connect better with my staff. I also collaborated with other leaders who seemed to have staff connection as their strength. My middle school leader Voxer PLN was excellent support along with leaders on Twitter.

I sought out a coach with a focus on growing my emotional intelligence as a leader which connected with the work we were doing as a school with students on social, emotional learning. My coach along with one of my district's middle principal school colleagues, helped me to identify some communication walls I had built that were getting in the way of my staff seeing that I valued them and served as my accountability partners to support my efforts. Along with implementing the strategies I was learning about through my reading and conversations, I did more listening, less talking, and was more judicious about not sharing my opinion when I just needed to ask questions.

Is my school community in a happily ever after? This isn't a Disney movie, so that is a no. However, my staff have commended my efforts and noted the difference it is making in our school community. I am no longer the challenge because I am actively working on balancing the expectations of being a good principal for all of my stakeholders.

Leading a building is about learning. You have to learn about your community, the needs of your students, and the strengths of your staff to implement a shared vision. This rewarding and challenging work requires us to be in constant reflection and open to being a student of ourselves and others. The challenges we face as principals will be many, but if we are committed to being a principal in action, we will commit to continuous growth like our staff and students to create communities where everyone feels connected and valued.

For Mark, this is his 37th year as an educator and 22nd as an elementary school principal. Being connected with other leaders across the country has revitalized Mark's attitude and energized his spirit. Mark has a group of colleagues who inspire, motivate, encourage, and hold him accountable. The challenges get Mark out of his office and connecting with students, teachers, food service team members, paraprofessionals, bus drivers, custodians, parents, and other stakeholders. Mark is excited to be a principal in action at this point in his career.

We challenge you to get out of your office and interact with your students and staff members. We encourage you to follow the #PrincipalsInAction hashtag and participate in the challenges. Find ways to share your experiences with your school community through your newsletter, blog, and social media accounts. Join the movement, get out of your office, and show others how much fun being a principal can be!

Challenge

Find the weekly challenge on Twitter at #PrincipalsInAction. Take a picture of the challenge and share it on Twitter or in our Voxer group. If you aren't on Voxer, sign up for it and connect with Mark (mfrenc221), Ryan (sheehyrw), or Jay (jposic498) to join the #PrincipalsInAction Voxer group. Weekly challenges are some of the best ways we have been able to help principals get out of their offices and they can help you get out of your office, too.

Chapter 4

Make Someone's Day

(Mark French)

A principal is the person who creates the climate and develops the culture in a school. Sometimes a principal needs to make decisions that change the ways that things have always been done. Change is difficult, and sometimes what a principal thinks is a minor change can be a pretty major thing for a student or a staff member. When these changes occur, the principal is often left on the outside of the parking lot or teachers' lounge conversations.

Have you ever felt this way?

We're sure that you have, and sometimes it's just someone reaching out to you, or you reaching out to someone else, that can change the course of your day right at the time that you need it. It is our job to lift each other up and look for the opportunity to make someone's day.

At the beginning of one school year, I received one of the greatest surprises I've ever had. One of my role models (someone I follow and connect with on Twitter, Facebook, and Voxer) and an educator who had reenergized my spirit, stopped by my school and surprised me as I was welcoming staff back for our first professional development day of the new school year. Adam Welcome, amazing and inspiring California educator, co-founder and co-author of *Kids Deserve It* and author of *Run Like a Pirate*, stopped by my school to surprise and meet me for the first time while on his way to central Minnesota for keynoting engagements. This speaks to the quality of this guy that he would take time out of his busy schedule to surprise me and make my day.

Now, I know we all cannot travel across the country to surprise each other like Adam was able to do, but there are other actions you can take to make someone's day.

- Pick up the phone and surprise someone with a call.
- Write a note to a colleague and include some of your school swag.
- Send an uplifting text message to GIF to brighten someone's day.

At a recent principals' conference I attended, the speaker had participants get up, connect with someone we didn't know, and tell them about one of our amazing staff members. Before we left, the speaker told us to capture the name and email address of the teacher we just heard their principal gush about and send them an email message telling them the great things their principal said. Talk about making someone's day!

Ryan looks for these opportunities every day. If Adam's

visit made me feel this way, Ryan thinks about the ways that he can make someone's day. There are days that Ryan walks campus passing out Skittles to teachers, telling them that he is just trying to put a smile on their face. People make Ryan's day all the time by doing little stuff. Whether receiving snail mail, a phone call, or a simple text message Ryan gets through each day it makes his day and puts a smile on his face. Get out of your office and make these simple gestures and the world becomes that much better.

Ryan also enjoys calling educators around the country just to chat and see how they are doing. Ryan called a school in New England one day because of some of the work he saw on Twitter. When the front office picked up the phone they transferred the call into the principal's office. Ryan said, "Good morning! This is Ryan Sheehy", and the other end of the phone went silent. The person Ryan called was shocked that Ryan had taken the time out of his day just to make a call. They went on to talk about all the great things happening in the school and how they were able to achieve that. Ryan makes a point that when he calls others that they talk about the positives and some struggles. This allows others to hear from a different perspective and allows Ryan to share with them any advice that has worked for him.

Jay has connected with a nearby principal in a different district, Dennis Griffin. Dennis is a younger administrator (he was 6 when Jay graduated from college) and both he and Jay speak to each other on the phone at least every other week and connect on Voxer almost daily. They talk about successes, struggles, school culture, leadership, academics, and behavior. The best part about this connection for Jay is that he learns more from Dennis than Dennis learns from him. Dennis reinvigorates Jay to be better for kids every day. It all started with a simple phone call, a connection that is great for Dennis and for Jay. These phone calls make Jay's day, and he hopes that they make Dennis' day, too.

You can make a phone call; write and send a note; text a photo; schedule a Google Hangout or Facebook Messenger video chat; send a heartfelt email; post a funny Tweet or direct message; leave a Voxer message; create and send a video; give a face-to-face greeting; and/or leave a treat on someone's desk, chair, or mailbox.

I remember the kind actions members of my PLN have taken the past couple of years. I have received cards, letters, notes, gift cards, wrist bands, t-shirts, stickers, drawings, phone calls, email messages, Twitter direct messages, Voxer messages, and visits, and I save and remember them all. You probably remember the things you have received from others and now it's time to pay it forward and make someone's day.

Challenge

Think about someone that you have connected with recently. Now reach out to them. Call them on the phone. Send them a text message. Invite them out for coffee or lunch or dinner. Invite them to an EdCamp or conference so that you can reconnect with them and get them connected with others.

Chapter 5

Make Connections and Build Your PLN

(Jay Posick)

Being a principal can be a lonely job.

There is no one else in a school that has the same job description as the principal. Ultimately, the principal is the person who makes the decisions that will impact all students, staff, and families. The principal can ask for advice from an assistant principal if they have one, but asking only someone in your school for advice can be limiting, and sometimes scary. Think about it. Who would feel completely comfortable asking someone in your school or district for advice? There can be that thought in the back of your mind that you are showing weakness or possibly disrespect, especially if you are questioning a decision that you need to implement.

Some schools have leadership teams and in some schools, the leadership team consists of one. If you don't have someone in your school or district to connect with, it's vital that you develop a professional or personal learning network. Not only will they encourage and support you, but they will also stretch you beyond your self-imposed limits.

When I began as a principal in 2007, I was the only administrator in my school. I had no assistant principal or dean of students, but I did have a very supportive superintendent. I had begun developing a PLN, but it was on a very small scale, consisting of mostly other Wisconsin administrators with similar experiences who were members of our state principals' association. Now that's not a bad thing at all, especially because I was new and needed to forge relationships with experienced principals.

Then, in January of 2010, I started to become connected using Twitter. The first two principals I met face to face after I joined Twitter is Curt Rees (@CurtRees) from LaCrosse, Wisconsin, and Jessica Johnson (@PrincipalJ) from Juneau, Wisconsin. The face to face connection led to presentations about being connected at our state principals' conventions and eventually joining Voxer. My PLN has grown exponentially since then because of the incredible educators I have become connected with both on Twitter and on Voxer. Another connection happened with Joe Sanfelippo (@Joe_Sanfelippo), a superintendent from Fall Creek, Wisconsin. Joe heard about the monthly assemblies I have in Merton and wanted to learn more about them. Joe and I connected on a Google hangout, my first ever, and we discussed the amazing opportunities that these monthly assemblies created.

These three connections, all with Wisconsin educators, have

allowed me to become connected with principals from Alaska to Massachusetts and all states in between. The incredible thing about the connections I have made is that when I talk on Twitter, Voxer, Google hangouts, or in person the issues I discuss are the same regardless of the state or community in which you live. The real constant in all of the connections I have made with others is that we are all educating students, staff, and one another.

The greatest connections I have made occurred within the last two years because I attended the National Principals' Conferences in Philadelphia and Chicago. Ryan, Mark, and I were fortunate to have presented together in Philadelphia, meeting for the first time in person the night before the conference. We had worked together on our presentation using Google slides and Google hangouts. I also had the opportunity to present with Don Gately, a middle school principal in New York City, meeting him in person for lunch before we presented. Don and I worked on our presentation via Google presentations, Google hangouts, and by phone. Two presentations in one day with principals from California, Minnesota, and New York. That's the power of connections!

I'm Not Lonely Anymore

J. Kapuchuck, Elementary Principal, Harrisonburg, VA

In my 21 years working in public education, I have had the opportunity to work with many administrators throughout my career. I have learned from each one of them and they all have had an influence on my personal educational journey. However, the one group that has had the greatest impact on my administrative career has been Principals In Action.

Being a principal is a twenty-four hour job that often feels lonely and overwhelming. You are responsible for your building, your faculty and staff, and the most important resource, your students. It is a gift to have colleagues to connect with worldwide to assist and support you as the leader in your building. I often find myself reaching out to Principals In Action for advice or wisdom on how to handle a complex situation or searching for ideas on how to better my school. Over 2,000 children's books were purchased and sent home with students, a Gaga pit was installed on our playground, a sensory path was created in our hallway, themed treat days for our staff and many other items have occurred in our building because of the ideas shared by different leaders involved in Principals In Action. By connecting with this group through various media forms like Twitter and Voxer, our school is a better place and the job of a principal does not seem so lonely anymore.

One of the Principals In Action mottos is to "Get out of your office." This is a great daily reminder that we need to be out in the building, on the playground, in the cafeteria, and connecting with our students. Being out of my office allows me to build stronger relationships with my students and gives me a better understanding of their individual needs. The students are often excited to share with me a school activity they are working on, read me a book, or tell me about something that is happening outside of school. I want to make sure my students know they are genuinely cared for and we are excited to see them each day they are in school. These relationships would not be built if I sat in my office each day and only came out to visit classrooms when it is time to complete an observation.

"Smiles, High Fives, and Changing Lives" is another important motto of Principals In Action. As a principal, I often discuss with our staff about creating memorable learning experiences for our students. I have had to step outside of my comfort zone many times in order to create these experiences and put smiles on the faces of my students. Getting slimed, silly-stringed while being duct-taped to a wall, rappelling off the school and a fire truck ladder, dressing up in costumes, and even parachuting from a plane when the students reached their fundraising goal were activities I never dreamed I would be doing when I became a principal. However, when you see the excitement and happiness these activities have brought to my students, I often think "What's Next?"

When Ryan was a physical education teacher he would travel from between school sites. Some years he had to travel to six different buildings. Each day was usually a different site and different staff. It was difficult, because Ryan never felt that he was part of a team plus it was difficult to form relationships on a one-day week cycle. Fast forward years later when Ryan took over as a high school vice principal. He was stepping into a role that he did not know and needed support. Ryan remembers purchasing tons of leadership books and looking for every resource possible. Listening to podcasts, reading books, and talking with other administrators he found helpful, but there was still a lack of PLN for administrators. It is lonely at the top and you need those people to bounce questions off of and just have a conversation with.

After two weeks of being a high school vice principal, Ryan was introduced to a platform that he believes changed his life. Ryan was introduced to Voxer, which is a walkie talkie app that allows you to connect with others from around the world without having anyone's phone number. This made connecting with others so much easier. Ryan joined different Voxer and Twitter groups/PLNs and started building relationships. Ryan continued building these relationships and they helped him overcome different hurdles that he encountered everyday on the job.

After two years of being a vice principal, Ryan landed a

building principal position at a local elementary school. The first year was full of adventure and changes. Within the first 60 days of the school year, there were instructional changes, investigations, and school tragedy that Ryan faced. Ryan remembers reaching out to his Principals In Action community for some help. Ryan had just escorted three staff members off the campus for differing reasons and faced a difficult investigation ahead of him. He remembers the outpouring of support and side messages that he received during this trying time. This job is not easy, but it is manageable and fulfilling when you surround yourself with amazing people that will help you get through difficult times or just need some advice.

Mark feels more vitalized and motivated at this point in his career than he did in the beginning and it is because of the networks, connections, and friendships made on social media. The connections started with a challenge from George Couros in December 2013 to connect with others through Twitter. Mark had a Twitter account for a few years before then, but was not using it to connect, learn, and share. Previously, Mark expanded his learning and connecting at national, state, and local conferences, but when those were over, so were the connections he made with others. Now, Mark has a PLN that he connects with daily and one that has supported him in positive and difficult times.

Challenge

If you are not on Twitter or Voxer, now is the time to join. Joining these, or other social media platforms will expand your circle of learning and influence. Follow #PrincipalsInAction for celebrations and questions, even if it is to lurk for a day, week or month.

Bonus Challenge

Follow someone new on Twitter and send them a direct message to set up a Google hangout to discuss a topic that you both have an interest in or about which you have questions. Be sure to post on Twitter using #PrincipalsInAction.

Chapter 6

How Do Teachers Feel About Having a Principal In Action?

(Jay Posick)

Being part of Principals In Action can be a big change for teachers and students. Unfortunately, many in education remember the stereotypical principal sitting in a sterile office, answering phone calls and emails, writing up reports and evaluations, and only visiting classrooms to find a student in trouble or to do a formal evaluation on a teacher. Principals In Action strive to change that stereotype and some of our teachers relish the visibility in the classroom.

I have a number of teachers who are on Twitter. They share their view of their classrooms and our school and are truly creating the story of the school that we want others to know about. One of our Merton teachers, Brian Klink (@brian_klink) tweeted this...

"My principal, @posickj, strives on being visible & is constantly in classrooms. Some would even say ninja-like how he just appears out of nowhere. Definitely changes the culture to "got your back" vs. the negative alternative. Isn't that how it should be?"

My favorite part of Brian's tweet is that he notices the change in culture to "got your back". That is so much better than a "gotcha" visit. Being in classrooms regularly allows you to see a much more normal view of classroom procedures and expectations. I learned this from my first principal in 1987, Mr. Joe Vitale. I remember him visiting my classroom early and often during my first year as a classroom teacher. Back in 1987, there was still mail that was regularly delivered to the school. Mr. Vitale would sit at a table in my classroom, go through his mail, write letters and notes to families and teachers, and watch me teach. He wasn't there as a "gotcha". He was there as a "got your back". I learned the importance of being in classrooms from Mr. Vitale, and even before *Principals In Action*, I visited classrooms as regularly as I could as a principal. Visiting classrooms has become a regular part of my school day. I visit as many of the classrooms as I am able each day. Some teachers will ask me to stay and help support them in their classrooms while others will invite me in to show them something new that they are trying or to get some suggestions for classroom procedures or student behaviors. These invitations would never happen if I seldom visited classrooms. The culture and climate of our school have definitely become one of "got your back" and not one of "gotcha".

When Ryan took over as an elementary principal he

followed someone that was definitely not a principal in action. She trapped herself in the office and when she did emerge, she did not interact with students or staff. Over the course of Ryan's first year on campus, teachers/students/community saw Ryan out and about with students and the community. He made it a point to be outside each morning, playing music and welcoming students, staff, and parents onto campus. This gave people a chance to connect with him and have conversations about things that they did not want to email or call him about.

About three months into the year a teacher approached Ryan. She asked if he had a few minutes to talk and they went into his office. As they were talking the teacher started mentioning her friend who had taken over at a school in a nearby city. As she was talking, she asked Ryan if it was okay to give him his number. She went on to say that he faced many of the same challenges that Ryan had but handled them in a different way and it didn't go so well. Ryan was willing to meet with the principal and help them out in any way possible.

After that conversation, Ryan knew that being a principal in action was working. His staff, his students, and his community had seen a difference and the community that once was divided was realigned back in support of students, no matter what it takes.

Before Mark connected with other principals in action, he tried to break the stereotype of a principal who sat in their office and waited for problems. He visited the playground, spent time in the cafeteria, stopped into classrooms, but really wasn't focused on developing relationships, learning and becoming better. Is Mark perfect? Absolutely not. He wants to spend more time in classrooms observing teaching and learning and finding ways to support teachers and students and he is working to get better at that.

When teachers first encounter a principal of action they are shocked. Unfortunately, throughout history, principals follow the stereotype and are not strong leaders when it comes to classrooms and students. This is something we need to change. A principal in action is not a title, it is something that is demonstrated all day, every day.

Here is one other point. Being a principal in action can be difficult for some of our staff. They will wonder why you aren't staying in your office. They will wonder why you are visiting classrooms. They will wonder why you stop by during their conferences. They will wonder why you stop into their room during a planning period to talk. How can you take the wonder away? Be upfront and transparent. Talk to the staff about why you aren't in your office. They need to know that being in classrooms, watching teachers and students in action, is why you aren't in your office. Connecting with students and staff in the hallways or before school or after school or at lunch is why you aren't in your office. And when families call the office, and you're not in your office, the secretary can tell them you're in classrooms with the students and staff. The missed phone calls can be returned later, and the emails can be answered later, but watching the learning in classrooms can only happen when the students and staff are in the building. So get out of your office and watch the learning happen.

He's here again.

Sarah Kasprowicz, Middle School Teacher, Merton, WI

He's here again. My principal is in my room. He's sitting next to Brandon and quietly reading a book. There was no advance notice nor any nervous murmurs from my sixth graders to announce his arrival. Am I startled? Nervous? No. It is normal. That's why no one made any sound. Nobody is worried and there is no cause for a ruckus.

Jay Posick is my principal and can often be found in my room reading or working right alongside my sixth graders. He's a little taller and his book might be a professional development text instead of the latest dystopian novel, but it isn't awkward because he is a part of our class. In fact, Jay is a part of every class in our school. That's what a Principal In Action does. They come to your classroom and participate.

Our students know that Mr. Posick is here for them because he takes the time to get to know them. He might ask them about the book their reading, or maybe he will ask how their hockey game went over the weekend. During tough conversations about poor choices at recess, he might ask them, "What could you have done differently?" Since our students trust their principal is a fair and caring person, they will actually answer him with a sincere alternative that they wish they would have done instead. Jay coaches basketball and volleyball, which gives him added insight into the dynamics our students are dealing with. Coaching also gives him additional time with our students to get to know them and be a mentor in a different way. That's what a Principal In Action does. They connect with their students and show that they care.

Jay was a teacher for many years and has never forgotten what it's like to be in the classroom. That's extra good for us because he teaches in our school a lot. Sometimes he teaches advanced math for our Geometry class, maybe it's seventh grade art or tomorrow he might be teaching fifth grade science because a teacher needs coverage. Then there is recess duty. A wise educator once told me that you can gauge the integrity of a principal by whether or not they do recess duty. Well, guess what. I don't have a massive winter recess jacket, but Jay does. He knows that being visible and accessible at recess every day reminds the students that he is always there with them and for them. It makes our students feel safe and valued that their recess time is worth their principal's time. It also reduces the number of fish stories we get about recess because, well, our principal was out there too and maybe that never happened.

Having a Principal In Action helps me as a teacher because when Jay and I discuss students, I trust his opinion because he knows the kids. Not just their name...he knows who they are, who they sit with at lunch and who they play with (or don't) at recess. He knows how they are doing in volleyball and whether or not they excel at art and maybe that's their outlet.

A Principal In Action knows that little things can make a big difference for his staff. This also helps me as a teacher because I am inspired because Jay believes in his teachers. Jay makes us feel appreciated by giving us handwritten thank you notes for being awesome in the classroom and he and his wife give us gifts and make us lunch for the holidays. Jay knows that teachers want to feel that they are doing a good job, so he goes that extra distance to provide encouragement for his staff to keep doing the best job they can every day. Jay arranges gift card raffles for staff during spirit week, which adds fun to our day and increases participation in Flannel Friday or Crazy 80s Day. When Jay knows that stress levels are creeping up he announces that tomorrow is Jeans Day. It sounds small, but it means a lot that Jay cares that we might want to relax tomorrow and throw on jeans instead of worrying about what we should wear. It's not about the jeans for me. These gestures help me as a teacher because my principal pays attention to how his staff is feeling and cares that we are comfortable. That's what a Principal In Action does. They create bright spots in our day to show they know we give our best every single day.

I am so grateful that Jay is a Principal In Action because he literally makes the school day tick, tock, and rock around the clock. He greets students and staff each morning with confident strides and a cheery hello while upbeat music plays from his "Jammy Pack" around his waist. Jay is there for us all day long and twice a week he stays until 5:15 in order to help students with their assignments at his Homework Club in the library. Teachers post to #MertonProud because our Principal iIn Action asks us to Tweet what our students are doing and he almost immediately shows his support with retweets. That's what a Principal In Action does. They curate positivity and champion our successes.

Jay is rarely in his office during school hours because he is where he wants to be and is most effective, which is with us. He does have a sign up on his office door and if you request it, he will meet you there. But otherwise, keep the office empty and keep the Principal In Action.

Challenge

Have a purposeful discussion with your staff about your reasons for being out of your office. Survey the staff to find those who would welcome more regular classroom visits and have this group of staff share their experiences with other staff members to grow a culture that celebrates having a principal in action who gets out of their office.

Chapter 7

Things They Don't Teach You in "Principal School"

(Jay Posick)

Imagine that you have just gotten your first principal job. Where do you even begin? Do you start by meeting all of the staff? Do you have a meet and greet with the community? Do you meet with the outgoing principal or the superintendent who hired you? It's a daunting responsibility and nowhere in your principal training did they really tell you what to expect. Honestly, the most amazing thing about being a principal is that you never know what the day will bring.

I barely remember my first real day as a principal. It was over 12 years ago. I started by having my first staff meeting, using a PowerPoint that I cannot even find anymore. I know that it included scenes from "Mr. Holland's Opus", a powerful film about how building relationships can have an impact on students and staff alike. But after that, it was a blur of meetings, conversations with staff, and trying to prioritize the never-ending list of items on my to-do list. I also knew that I had to be ready for my first open house that would be a few days later. As I said, I barely remember that first day, but it did consist of lots of relationship building and lots of listening.

First days only happen once a year, but so do second days, and third days. You get the point. In each of these days, something will likely occur that you weren't told about in principal school. I've gone dumpster diving for retainers. I've been slimed as part of a fundraiser. I've captured a dog and returned it to its owner, only to be zapped by the electric collar when I walked into the owner's yard. I've been hugged on stage by a student at graduation, and the student wasn't even my own child. I end our daily announcements with this one line, "Make it the best {insert day}of the week." It has become my tag line in the Voxer groups I'm in. Just think of the message that's being sent. Today is the only day we know we have. Yesterday is gone and tomorrow isn't promised to us. It's so important for us to put our focus on today.

Ryan had a different path to becoming a principal. He actually never went through a program to become a principal. In the state of California, there was a time period where you could take a test to get your administrative credential. Ryan was able to study for, take and passe the six-hour exam. Ryan originally felt at a disadvantage when he started his principalship and was faced with different issues. While an administrator in a high school, no one had ever taught Ryan how to handle different social-emotional issues that arose commonly or how to break up a fight where students could get severely hurt. Ryan always took the approach that "Principal

School" was showing up each day and seeing what might happen. There is never two days of the same thing.

Mark was in "Principal School" a very long time ago when the role of the principal is different than today. Mark wasn't taught the importance of establishing and building relationships, the power of making connections, creating your Professional Learning Network, or how important it is to be a visible leader. Being a principal today is more about leading and managing people than it is about leading and managing a building. Your assets are your students, family members, and staff members, not the sparkling hallways, impressive cafeteria, auditorium or gymnasium, or your new school building. Mark knows that he is not perfect and sometimes needs to be reminded about the needs of the people he supports, but it is always right to focus on the people rather than the paperwork and email messages.

The Things They Didn't Teach You in "Principal School"

Dennis Griffin, Principal, Brown Deer, WI

Congratulations!!! You have done it. The vision that you have developed and refined in your mind over countless hours of reflection is becoming a reality. You are the principal. Relationships, Relationships, Relationships!!! You vividly remember that you need to develop relationships with members of your staff, parents, community members, and most importantly students. You remember that relationships are built on trust.

One of the first things that you do upon receiving your appointment is to schedule time to meet with your staff. You ask them to tell you about themselves. You ask, what is going well? What would you change? Tell me about the students? It was stressed to you that the first impression must count if you are going to be successful in your role. You know the moment the educator and parents leave you they are going to share their thoughts about you with members of the community. As a matter of fact, after each encounter, you might even play out in your mind what different people in the community are saying about you. You remember from your training that you are the instructional leader, the effective communicator, the problem solver, the financial officer for your institution, a champion for kids, and the list continues to go on and on.

And then it happens... You find yourself in a situation that you have never experienced and that your classroom experience did not prepare you for. Here are a few things that you might discuss in your coursework but will not completely grasp until you have experienced it.

Relationships Are Cultivated and Tested With Time

Building relationships that are based on trust are cultivated with time. Yes, the first impression is very important to start the relationship off on the right foot, however, every interaction after that is an opportunity to invest in relationships. Many principals will tell you that year two of the journey is one of the most challenging years within schools (they don't tell you this in school) and here is why, the first year, everyone is trying to figure each other out. People want to hear what your vision is (notice I said hear because you haven't necessarily taken any action steps at this time). People want to know what do you stand for as a leader. In year one, you are learning the climate, culture, and history of the school. In year two, everyone will look to see if your actions truly align with the words and the vision you set forth in year one. The more that you invest in your people, the greater level of trust and grace will be bestowed upon your relationships and leadership.

When cultivating trust remember that relationships are not friendships, however, friendships can develop over time. Think of collegial and congenial. Get Out of Your OFFICE!!! The real magic happens in classrooms. Trust is created there. Classroom visits should happen daily, not yearly. The Open Door Policy should exist for every room in the school. This includes feedback. Also, visit educators and families before school. Finally, know the aspirations of your staff and community. Trusting relationships allows others to help create and embrace the vision of the school

Conflict Is Inevitable

If you asked many people their take on the conflict they will tell you that they do not like it. As a matter of fact, most people try their best (or at least it seems) to avoid conflict. The problem is that conflict is inevitable. It is inevitable because our lives are in a constant state of change. The nature of change itself will pose various obstacles. This is due in large part because the problems we face today are from yesterday's solutions (Senge 1990). There is a tendency to want to keep a sense of routine within our lives and change disrupts that routine and predictability. When you are leading, challenges are supposed to test your capacity to serve as an agent of change.

Here are a few things to remember:

- Doing what is right is not always easy.
- Leading change is often uncomfortable but necessary.
- The risk of the journey itself creates conflict.
- What you Ignore You Validate!!!
- Have someone you can connect with.
- You will make mistakes. When they are made you have two choices: learn from them or repeat them.

Change/Fear of Loss

Experiencing loss is a difficult task because there are times that we allow our positions to get too close to our egos (Powell 2012). Within the change process, many educators will experience loss in some capacity. This can be the loss of a position, power, status, or even a classroom. On many accounts when the loss does not impact us directly we minimize it or at times do not even realize the loss because it and not intended to take place.

Always keep these tips top of mind... your position does not define you, your actions do. All loss is personal. Try not to minimize the impact that loss creates for another person. To venture into the unknown is initially scary. Create new opportunities for everyone to use their multiple intelligences and talents

The Improvement Plan

In school, you discuss the possibility of putting an educator on a plan of improvement. You spend most of that time talking about how important documentation is, and making sure that you talk to the human resources department about action steps. I hate to say this but this is part of the job. The part that is not discussed is the physical and mental toll that this can have on you and the organization. When you place someone on a plan of improvement most of the time it is a very challenging ordeal. We are talking about a person's livelihood. You even begin to think about how will they support their families. You question if you did everything in your power to support them? Your decisions must be based on the fact that every student deserves the best educator in front of them. This impacts climate temporarily and the culture forever. How it impacts the culture will be determined by your relationships. This process will hurt because of relationships that exist within the organization. Relationships will be tested. Fear of this could happen to me may surface from others

Problems

I never believe in obstacles. I believe that every obstacle is an opportunity in disguise. It does not make the obstacle any less daunting of a task, it is just a mindset of growth. When it comes to problems there are a few things that every principal needs to remember. First, every problem ultimately is your problem, but that does not mean it is your problem to solev. Sometimes it is better to ask the right questions when seeking a solution. Once you do so, empower your teacher leaders to help solve problems and help them reflect on the process. Refelction is the key to leveragig problems to create or promote growth.

Let's face it, without probelems how do you knwo what type of leader you are much less teh type of leaders you are developing? Leadership is not always clear skies and sunny days. Leadership is hard work, but it is worth it.

Politics

Bolman and Deal (1991) discussed the four frames that are present in organizations. The area that I had to grow the most in was the political frame. I had to learn that every decision that I made in my role as a principal, educator, or even as a father would be interpreted through a political lens that others often used to define who I was as a person. Remember to:

- Always remember your "WHY".

- Be authentic.

- Create transparency and consistency.

- Try not to take it personally.

- Understand your decisions have an impact that at times may not be intentional.

Study Leadership

Your journey of learning does not end with your graduation or acceptance of your assignment as the principal of the school. On many accounts, we are continuing to enhance our instructional leadership within the confines of our schools. Something that should also be considered is that is imperative that principals continue to study and learn about leadership. There is a wealth of knowledge and resources that discuss the topic of leadership. Studying leadership helps to provide insights on how to help navigate meaningful change within an organization. If you want to differentiate between a leader and a manager ask them to create meaningful change (Maxwell 1994).

Studying leadership for me happens in several ways. You coudl read leadership books and articles. Next, connect with leaders on twitter and Voxer to build your professional learnign network. Find and develop relationships with mentors you can trust. By having mentors and a stron

PLN, you can have probelem solving sessions with these groups as well as be a particpant in you rPLN's problem solving sessions.

Prepare Your Family

The greatest mistake that I made when I became a principal was that I did not prepare my family for my new role. They were excited when they realized that I had accomplished my goal of becoming a principal. What they did not understand, was the difference it would make in my schedule. I went from being at every event to not always being in the stands. Conflicting schedules became the norm. I did not understand how the thoughts of others would impact my family and not just me.

Your schedule will change, but be sure to keep your family as your number one priority. Help your family understand the role of the principal as well as the good and the bad aspects of leadership. Your family will get defensive if they hear people talk poorly of you as they feel the joy and pain of your leadership journey. It's important ot learn to unplug. Allow your family to help create your work/life balance

To this day, I remember when my superintendent told me that I can put in for vacation days during the Spring and Winter breaks. I asked him what did he mean. He stated that I was a twelve month employee. To this day the two of us still get a laugh out of that moment. Initially, I did not know how to negotiate my salary or the terms of my contract. I did not know about the process that was utilized to evaluate principals. I had to learn about the importance of developing frameworks and systems to help the school function without allowing the system to define who we were (Blanchard, 2018). There are many aspects of the principalship that are not necessarily covered in your administration classes and honestly, I can not cover all of them here.

The last thing that I will share is that you made the right decision. You have a desire to serve as an agent of change in spite of the human desire to hold fast to the status quo. You have a vision of a better tomorrow and are willing to engage collaborative teams to not only identify, but create solutions that will essentially create the next set of obstacles. Being a principal is the most rewarding vocation I can imagine and I wouldn't change my decision for the world.

Challenge

Share a story about something that has happened to you as a principal that you never knew could happen. How did you handle the situation? Who did you turn to for ideas or support, or did you just try to handle the situation on your own? If you are comfortable, share the story using the #PrincipalsInAction hashtag.

Chapter 8

Being Flexible

(Jay Posick)

I believe the best part of being a principal is that you have a chance to set your schedule. I also believe the best part of being a principal is that your schedule isn't your schedule. Not every principal might feel the way that I do. As an educator, one needs to be able to think on their feet, make adjustments, and be available for just about anything. Principals never really know what to expect from day to day. That's not to say that teachers or other educators really know what to expect from day to day, either. They don't. It's just that they have a schedule that they must follow with their students, sometimes involving bells and sometimes not, but it is more of a structure than a principal might have. The need to be flexible is critical for a principal because if their schedule has any openings, there's a good chance that someone, or something, will want to fill those openings.

I know it sounds counterintuitive to have a calendar that

is mine as well as the school's, but it is vital to have these two schedules. Being a principal requires being exceptionally flexible. I have found that if I put it on my calendar, it gets done. But my calendar isn't filled every day. There are lots of spots for flexibility. Honestly, the only scheduled item on my calendar every day is lunch and recess duty. The rest of my days are very flexible. If nothing is on my calendar, I'm in classrooms.

With flexibility comes opportunity to be in classrooms, hallways, the cafeteria, the playground, and the roof (someone has to get the playground balls off the roof). There is also the opportunity to speak with the family members of our students and staff, all sorts of staff, and community members.

I use Google calendar for the reminder function but I also have a calendar on my office door. Staff, students, and our secretary can see where I might be or where I might have an opening to meet. When I do stop by my office, I check my door calendar to see if anyone has signed up to meet with me. Any new appointments are put into my Google calendar and are then highlighted on my door calendar. That's how I can tell when a new appointment has been added to my door calendar. Like I said earlier, if it's on my door calendar it will be added to my Google calendar and that means it's going to happen. Sometimes I put another sign on my door.

If you're looking for me, just wait! I'll be in
your room in no time. If it's an emergency,
text me, email me, or tweet me (@posickj).
IT'S A NO OFFICE DAY!
#PRINCIPALSINACTION

I might only have this sign up on my door once a month, but it's one of my favorite days. Sometimes I leave my Chromebook in my office and just take my phone. I need my phone on these days for two purposes- to take pictures in classrooms and to be available for a text from our secretary in case I'm needed in the office. What better way to learn about your school than to spend the day out of your office.

Flexibility is the key to success in all areas of education. Ryan has had to be extremely flexible throughout all of his education career. As a teacher, things were thrown his way on a regular basis and being rigid was not a possibility. If he was not flexible, Ryan would have gone insane. Now as a principal, Ryan feels that he may have many things on his calendar, but other things come up. These things inlcude behaviors, meetings, and classroom observations that may need attention. When these things come up, other things will have to fall off of the calendar for a short time. The thought of this for many gives them anxiety. The reality is that without the right mindset about flexibility, individuals quickly get burned out.

One of the standards on the formative evaluation system Mark uses with his teachers is "Demonstrating Flexibility and Responsiveness." Mark observes, comments on, and provides feedback on this standard to teachers who respond to students' interests, spend more time on topics as needed, and find other ways to deliver instruction that wasn't planned. Principals need to demonstrate flexibility and responsiveness as well. If a playground/cafeteria supervisor is out sick, do you step in and help supervise? If a staff member needs to come in late or leave early for something, will you fill in for them?

If a parent stops by unexpectedly, is your schedule flexible enough to meet, listen, and help? Demonstrating flexibility and responsiveness shows you are willing to do whatever is needed whenever it is needed. However, like Ryan and me, Mark believes in scheduling things into his calendar. Mark could have the best intentions, but if it isn't scheduled, then it's not likely to happen. Mark schedules classroom read-alouds, classroom visits, playground supervision, formative observations, and formative observation write-ups into his calendar to make sure they happen.

Challenge

Can you use your calendar to schedule commitments while leaving open time to respond to things as they arise?

Bonus Challenge

Share your calendar with your administrative assistant to help you by scheduling appointments and commitments. Share your calendar with your supervisor so they can see how you are being a principal in action out of your office.

Chapter 9

Getting Out of Your Office

(Jay Posick)

The mantra of Principals In Action is "Get Out Of Your Office". It's on our wristbands as a reminder. Most of our challenges are centered around principals getting out of their offices. But looking at a wristband or taking on a challenge doesn't always create the daily habit of being out of your office. The daily habit of getting out of your office is created by getting out of your office. Sounds easy, doesn't it? But sometimes other things get in the way.

The unexpected visit from a student, staff member, or family member of a student happens. There's a red light on your phone that means someone left you a voicemail. There are the five, ten or twenty emails that appear in your inbox that weren't there only a minute ago. There's the visit from the district office that then requires you to provide a report for a meeting you didn't know you were going to have that afternoon. You might need to fill in for a teacher who suddenly became ill and there is no one else to cover their class (This one really counts as getting out of your office but still limits the places that you can visit.).

Paperwork, emails, phone calls and safety plans often occupy the minds of principals on a daily basis. The times where principals sit in their office and respond to phone calls, emails, and complete paperwork all day are over. We have reached the time in education, with all the different things on our leaders' plates, that if we do not spring into action, we will lose our enthusiasm and our rapport with the people we serve, our kids and staff.

Although time is needed in your office to complete paperwork, there are other times and ways to get paperwork and managerial tasks completed. You can work on paperwork before or after school. But you can get the paperwork done during school, too. In the age of Chromebooks and other personal devices, paperwork can also be done while you visit classrooms. Being a principal in action doesn't mean that the paperwork and managerial tasks don't get done; they just happen to get done either when the students and staff aren't in school or it gets done with a mobile office.

As you begin making this habit a priority, there may be some who are questioning why you are visiting classrooms or hanging out in the hallways or avoiding your office. They may ask you how you're getting all of your "principal work" done if you're not in your office. I would argue that the real "principal work" is getting into classrooms to see what learning is really going on. If you visit classrooms, the teachers and the students begin to expect it. I have made it such a habit that I visit an average of 20 classrooms a day out of the 27 classrooms in our school. If I don't visit a classroom, the teachers, and sometimes the students, ask me where I was. I'm invited into classrooms to see activities, to listen to presentations, to do read-alouds, and even to join in review games. One of our teachers uses the Circle of Power and Respect in his classroom and he often invites me to be a part of this amazing relationship building activity. If I'm not in classrooms and I'm not interacting with students and staff on a daily basis, I believe I don't really know what's happening in our school. And if I'm not interacting with students and getting to know them, there's no way I'd be invited into a Science classroom to do the Circle of Power and Respect (CPR). To do CPR right, you need to know your classmates (if you're a student) and students (if you're an educator).

I am rarely in my office but I have access to many forms of communication with my mobile technology. Our school secretary can reach me at any time by texting me. I can quickly check my phone and know whether I am needed immediately or where I might need to go to help with a student issue. When I leave the main office, I let our school secretary know where I'm going so that she is aware. It just makes things easier for her so she knows where I am in case a staff member or student might need to find me. I also have a Chromebook so I can check and respond to email messages or provide feedback when I am in class. One big advantage of being out of my office is that I can spread the good news of what's happening in our school through the use of social media, in particular Instagram, Facebook, and Twitter. If I'm walking around the building, going from classroom to classroom, it doesn't take much for me to take a picture with my phone and post it to social media while I'm moving on to the next classroom. If I am just sitting in my office, I really have little idea what's going on in our school. So you may be asking, "Jay, how can you be out of your office for most of the day?" The answer for me is a simple one and it's actually a question right back at you. "Why wait in your office for situations to come to you when you can get out of your office and meet the situations head on?"

Aside from having a mobile office, I am also a big part of our morning student drop off, lunch and recess duty, and afternoon student pick up. At times I may be the crossing guard or another adult on a bus ride. I have helped serve students during lunchtime and have been the health room aide, too. Assisting a custodian with a spill or fixing a ceiling tile (I used to do interior construction work) or clearing a sidewalk of snow are other ways I help out. Being involved in the school in a variety of ways sets an example for our students and staff. Helping out shouldn't be an imposition. It should be an opportunity. Get out of your office and get into action!

For Mark, being an active principal means getting out of his office, engaging with stakeholders, seeing how things are going, and finding ways he can be more supportive and helpful. Last year, he spent every day outside at recess and in the cafeteria supervising fifth graders. Being active allowed him to see how the grounds and equipment were being treated, pay attention to and improve transitions to the playground and cafeteria, mentor and collaborate with his playground/cafeteria supervisors, and observe how students interacted and treated each other. Mark wouldn't have received that big picture perspective if he were not out of his office being an active principal. Leaders need to be active and observing hallways, carpool drop off lanes, bus arrival, breakfast service, recess, lunchtime, and dismissal processes to see what's working and what can be improved.

Before arriving to his current school, Ryan's predecessor lived in their office. Teachers and staff made many comments to him about how she was always in her office and the door was closed. Ryan knew that needed it to change. Ryan lives in classrooms and often sets up an office in the back for the day in order to make sure that the paperwork and managerial tasks get done and the work doesn't pile up too much. Ryan also values the time of just being in classrooms interacting with students and learning alongside them. Too often when leaders come into classrooms to just work, things don't shift other than the workspace.

Getting into action is a choice that Ryan has made and is something that has changed his classrooms and instructional practices throughout the school. By being present in the rooms and on the playgrounds it has shown students where the priorities are for the school and the direction that they are heading. Being present and participating in lessons has given teachers a trust of Ryan that otherwise would have taken much time to gain. Professional development and meetings align to exactly what is going on in the classroom and that is all done by getting into action.

Finding a Champion

Curt Slater, Elementary Principal, Wyoming, MN

We have all heard the statement "It can be very Lonely at the Top." When I first started as a building principal, I found myself feeling that way on a daily basis. Not only was I lonely, but I was frustrated with my job and role as an elementary principal. When I work with kids I have always lived by the words of Rita Person, "Every Child deserves a champion: an adult who will never give up on them, who understands the power of connection and insists they become the best they can possibly be." The problem is that when I became a principal I found that I did not have a "Champion" in my professional life and I started to doubt myself. We all know what happens when people start to doubt themselves, we are not doing our best work and life becomes very stressful. I knew that something needed to change for me or I was going to have to find another profession.

My professional life changed when I connected with my Digital Professional Learning Community (DPLC) and the Principals In Action gang on Twitter, Voxer and Facebook. I was not isolated anymore, I found that many of the same struggles or issues that I was dealing with, other principals around the country are dealing with the same issues and when we work as a team to collaborate around those issues we made better decisions for our students, staff and community. We no longer can say, "It is lonely at the top" because we have the choice to connect, learn, collaborate and grow with others. Each week I look forward to the Principals In Action challenge, will I be serving lunch to students, riding a bus home, being a DJ on the playground or just finding a way to balance my work life with my personal life. I am motivated every day to get better because I am connected with other principals that are trying new and better ways to lead, learn and grow as leaders. The past 14 years I have trained and worked with schools around the Midwest to support

Positive Behavior Intervention Support (PBIS) and we are always looking at ways to build stronger positive relationships with our students, staff and families. #PrincipalsInAction is not only supporting leaders to make a positive change in their school it is breaking the mold of principals. We have the ability as leaders to create a better environment for all, it is time to break the old school mold of a principal and get out of your office smile, give high fives, and change lives!

The office can be a hideaway for some principals and, to be honest, sometimes it's necessary to be in your office for meetings or to personally regroup or to eat lunch. But don't let your office become the only place you do your work. You can complete paperwork and managerial tasks in classrooms, in the library, in the main office, or in the cafeteria.

Do principals need their office? Sometimes. Should their office be the only place they are seen? Absolutely not.

Challenge

Pick one "office task" to do outside of your office for a week. Reflect on whether doing this task outside of your office was negatively, neutrally, or positively impacted by not being in your office. If it was either neutrally or positively impacted, share it with us using the #PrincipalsInAction hashtag.

Chapter 10

Having Fun

(Mark French)

Lions and Tigers and Bears, oh my! In my case as an elementary principal it's been Ocelots, Roadrunners, and Gators, oh my! (Those were and are the mascots of the schools I have served as principal). Principals need to get out of their offices and be silly, promote the school, build a positive culture, and connect with students.

Throughout my administrative career, I've had fun by wearing our mascot costumes and other silly get-ups. I've worn our mascot costume at school open houses, family fun nights, during lunchtime, to honor a bet I made with students, and during school celebrations. I've also dressed as Zero the Hero; Mrs. Trunchbull from Matilda; book characters; a pirate for professional development and Talk Like a Pirate Day; Halloween characters (Harold's Purple Crayon, Waldo, Horton, The Mad Hatter, Curious George, Scarecrow, Pirate, and Max from Where the Wild Things Are). Being an active principal, putting yourself out there, and having fun contributes to a positive school climate and lets your school community see another side of you as the principal.

One of Jay's favorite things to do is to take part in Student Senate sponsored Spirit Weeks. Crazy hair days, dress up days, hat days (He wears a different one every hour of the day), pajama days- you name it and he's done it. The students and the staff see it as school spirit, even if it might be a little silly to see a grown person wearing pajamas during a parent meeting or family tour. As part of school fundraisers, Jay has also agreed to be slimed, get his head shaved, be duct taped to the wall, and get dunked in a dunk tank when it was 45 degrees. All of these activities show the fun side of Jay's personality.

If the principal has school spirit and shows it in fun ways, even if you're a secondary principal, why wouldn't others want to show their school spirit, too?

Ryan looks for any opportunity to have a good time with students. During Ryan's first year his parents club came to him with some wild ideas. They said that he was their choice at the interview because they knew that he would have fun and they had big plans on ways to create incentives for kids to learn, to raise money, and to make the school a better place. Ryan has enjoyed dressing up for spirit days, playing at recess, being turned into an ice cream sundae, being slimed, pied in the face, duct taped to the wall and so much more. The first time that Ryan participated in a spirit event of this type, a teacher came up to him and told him that she completely disagreed with the premise of students being allowed to pie the principal. To her, it was disrespectful and rude of kids. She didn't see the point to Ryan trying to build a culture of allowing students and teachers to have fun at school. Ryan frequently reminds educators that if we do not model that education is fun, then who would want to grow up to be an educator.

Think about ways in which you can participate in school spirit days, grade level activities, or just by playing with students at recess. You might also think about, schedule, and collaboratively plan days and activities that the entire staff, or student body, can participate in. A principal in action can also "spice up" and add fun to staff meetings and professional development sessions.

Redefining the Role of Principal

Miguel Castillo, Elementary Principal, Laredo, TX.

My memory that I have of my principal was that of someone I never knew until I got in trouble. He was the disciplinarian and someone we had to fear. I remember them, but for the wrong reasons. Even as a teacher, I remember the principal as someone who was always in the office and I would only see him when I needed to be evaluated.

The role of principal has evolved since I first taught 25 years ago. As the role has changed with accountability, principals are now instructional leaders. As instructional leaders, we need to inspire, lead, cheer, teach, support, and be the overall academic leader of the campus. However, the role of principal or instructional leader doesn't stop at the gates of the campus, but goes into the community. The principal represents the school and community where the school is located. The principal is an extension of the school and the district and as such, the principal is the instructional leader of the community even outside of the school.

The first time I heard the words "Principals In Action" was almost two years ago on Twitter from the innovative principal Mark French. I joined Twitter in 2016 and was looking for different ways to improve our school climate and culture. As I slowly learned and connected with other principals across the nation, I noticed that almost all the effective schools were doing some kind of actions that were unique and out of the ordinary. Each school was unique and each campus was led by a fun, energetic, funny, and caring leader

A Principal In Action, from my perspective, is an instructional leader who is innovative and thinks outside the box to create a positive climate that leads to a great school culture with high standards where all students learn in a positive and safe environment. One thing in common among Principals In Action is that they praise and recognize students, staff and parents. At our high-performing campus, Antonio M. Bruni Elementary in Laredo, Texas, students are recognized through the #GoodNewsCallOfTheDay, which was borrowed from @PrincipalFrench. Students are recognized with a picture frame, parents are called and they are given a certificate. This is one of the best actions that has helped our school climate. On certain occasions, students are encouraged to dress depending on the theme. For example, on the 80th day of school, students and staff can dress in 80's attire. To promote the love of reading through Accelerated Reader or AR, we designate a week with different themes each day and students can wear crazy hats, dress in safari to hunt for a good book, be a super reader and dress as a superhero, etc. During Read Across America and Dr. Seuss Birthday, students and staff can dress as characters from Dr. Seuss's books. The intent is for students to become engaged using innovative ways to promote the love of school and learning.

For staff, this year we started recognizing them by mugging them with a mug of goodies. We hashtag tag them with #bethedifference and #bethechange. We also use a picture frame and the school leadership team joins me to surprise the staff member. Another way that we appreciate staff is by providing coffee with pastries, taquitos, or treats once in a while. Staff enjoy the joy of being appreciated. We also treat our staff in May during teacher's appreciation week and throughout the year. It's not always about the treats for staff, but you have to be compassionate and empathetic with their needs. A Principal In Action is one that listens to the needs and understanding of staff.

A principal in action is also one that goes beyond the school and appreciates and values the community and parents. As a Title I schoolwide campus, we use some of our funds to provide ESL classes to our parents. We use this to promote parental engagement and teach our parents how to become more involved with their children in school. Once a month, different topics are covered and meetings are provided at different times to be flexible with our parents. As leader of the community school, a principal should care about the community it serves. One of the initiatives we have at our campus is the block walk. Before school starts, I take the lead teachers, administrative staff, and support staff to walk with me and visit some of our student's homes before school starts. Some of our parents and students are surprised and elated that we take the time to visit them at their humble homes and have coffee with sweet bread. Doing the block walks also shows our staff our community to better understand our students and where they come from.

At the end of the day, a principal in action should base every decision that is made, benefits the overall academic success of students. Sometimes it's not easy and may go against staff wishes, but if the decision benefits the child, the right choice was made. It may seem like fun and by all means, a principal should enjoy his or her role as the instructional leader of a campus, but sometimes it is not like that. There is one thing, and perhaps the most important factor that cannot be delegated to anyone, but the principal: accountability. The school's academic accountability rests solely on the leadership of the principal. There is a quote from Richard Marcinko that says, "Popularity is not leadership". While it may true, instructional leadership certainly doesn't have to be boring either.

Challenge

Be an active participant in your school's next spirit week, showing that you're a leader in school spirit and a leader for the school. Post a picture on Twitter using the hashtag #PrincipalsInAction.

Chapter 11

Create a Team

(Ryan Sheehy)

Whether you are working in business or education, workforce teams play a huge part in the success of the organization. Education is no different and often it seems that the team at a school plays more of a role in whether that school is successful or not. Every day this group of individuals comes together and hopefully shares a common goal and strives to meet the goal while making sure that everything else is taken care of and things are running smoothly.

I was a physical education teacher at an elementary school for ten years of my teaching career. One of the things that I missed most about being an elementary physical education teacher was being part of a team, being part of a tribe. I was part of the school staff but I didn't have a department. I didn't have people that I could bounce ideas off of. I didn't feel connected with any staff. I didn't have the time to connect with other educators at my site because I traveled between sites each and every week. When I taught middle school, I had a department there with three other physical education teachers. We were able to bounce ideas off each other and build upon the things that we learned together. When I transitioned back into the elementary physical education world from middle school I knew that would be the thing that I would miss most.

When I moved into the leadership role of the school, my team was about to change. As a vice principal, I had other vice principals and a principal to discuss challenges and changes. Even if it was my decision to make, it was nice to have someone with whom to discuss these ideas. My goal was to make every teacher, every educator, every staff member at my site feel like they were part of a team. Making others feel that they are an integral part of the team gives others confidence, boosting work production.

Once I was named principal, I set out to ensure that everybody knew they were part of my team and I was there to coach, guide, and do whatever it took to make things happen. Through using different technological tools such as Voxer, Twitter, and Instagram, I found a team. The team was there to push me to be stronger. Principals in Action is a Voxer group that started off with one goal and one goal only. The goal was to push every principal to get out of their office and start being with kids. A motto was created: Smiles/ High Fives/And Changing Lives.

As a parent, I watch my kids go through tryout after a tryout for different sports teams and I think about the interview process. Our interviews in education should be tryouts. We're looking for teachers, for educators, for staff members who are in school to be their best each and every day for our kids. It is our job as the leaders of the building to ensure that her teams have extra chemistry, they work hard together, and they function as a team. Education is a team sport just like life is a team sport. Together we can make everything amazing.

While developing a school team, it is important to find interview questions that get to more than just content knowledge. The questions should also get to the heart of relationships, character, and personality. We all have set up interviews based upon paperwork that we receive from candidates. Lately, Jay has added a video component to the interview process. The paperwork doesn't tell the entire story and neither does the video, but putting them both together can help us to bring in the best candidates for our openings.

When it's time for the interview, here are some questions to ponder.

1. What does it mean to you to be an educator in action?
2. If you were a breakfast cereal, what breakfast cereal would you be and why?
3. What non-professional book are you reading now and what has it taught you about yourself?
4. What role will you serve on your teaching team?
5. What ways will you get to know your students, colleagues, and families?
6. Who is the educator you remember most fondly? How will you be like that educator?
7. Who is in your personal learning network and why?
8. What is your favorite first activity of school for students?

Jay has found ways to help facilitate team building that helps the school be more like a family. They meet weekly with an agenda that always starts with kids. It is vital that they all see that the kids are the reasons we are educators. They share successes and struggles, finding ways to celebrate our successes while working together to find ways to handle their struggles. Additionally, if a staff member brings up a struggle they are having with a student or a struggling student, the staff member also needs to bring some possible solutions to deal with the struggle. Jay finds that having the staff member think of solutions helps the team focus on the solution instead of celebrating the struggle. The team approach to their kids is the reason they work together so well.

For Mark, creating a team means finding ways for staff members to come together to support the mission and vision. This can be challenging with a wide variety of employees in schools: licensed teachers, licensed support staff, clerical, health services, paraprofessionals, food service, custodial, bus drivers, etc. Mark has worked to find ways to recognize all employees (notes home; Grateful Gator Award; thank-you luncheons; coffee and donuts on a cart) and not just classroom teachers. You need to be a Principal In Action and connect with all staff members. Get out of your office and into the kitchen, cafeteria, playground, custodial office, parking lot, office area, classrooms, media center, gymnasium, all spaces at your school. Also, find ways, even if it is sporadic or once a year, to have all staff members come together. Mark works to invite and compensate non-licensed staff members to participate in their opening professional development day to reconnect, set the tone, and learn how each of us plays a role in supporting our mission.

Another important thought to consider is how teams are created. All staff should be given an opportunity to represent their grade level or content area. If you have the same people on every committee, you are only getting their voice. It's vital to get the voices of all staff. Some will agree with what's being discussed while some will not. Those conversations have an important influence on what we should do to move forward. If all have a voice, that can be beneficial. Listen to your staff, take their input, and make the changes that you all feel will benefit the school or organization.

Challenge

Check in with one of your teams about a recent decision that was made and the positive and negative outcomes of this decision. Determine together whether this decision needs to be changed or improved upon. Share this with your staff as a model of reflecting on school wide decisions.

Chapter 12

How to Stay Motivated

(Ryan Sheehy)

Being a member of a district team or PLN allows you to have conversations with other educators and hear how they feel about different trials and tribulations in the field. Education is hard and often we as educators get overwhelmed and lose the motivation and positivity that is needed all year long with our kids. There is no time to get stuck in a dark place with negative thoughts about our schools and our kids. We must constantly fight that feeling and look for ways to keep the motivation and positivity alive.

How do you keep yourself motivated?

How do you foster a positive attitude?

Most educators deal with lack of motivation or positivity at some point in their career. What it comes down to is how will that combat that and move forward, making sure that they are doing what is best for kids along the way.

As I work with different educational leaders and we work together through their struggles or areas that they want to improve upon, those questions of motivation and attitude always come up. A variety of answers are given and typically it has something to do with kids, which is the reason we get into education. As I talked with an Instructional Coach she began to talk about some major roadblocks that she was facing. Different personnel situations had made it very hard for her to do her job and change the way instructional was being delivered. Her time was being diverted away from instruction and into a black hole that many of us face in educational leadership. Before addressing the roadblock, I asked her the motivation questions. She sat there in silence for a few minutes before she could formulate an answer. She began to explain that she didn't have any particular way, but when she was lacking focus or motivation, she liked just laying in her bed. This brings up the need for intentionality when it comes to maintaining motivation.

On a different occasion, a principal was going through some rough things with her staff. She was a first year principal that had been challenged with many different issues concerning her staff. She began the year extremely motivated and ready to tackle the world. By winter break, she was frustrated and had lost some of the "ready to take on the world mentality", which was totally understandable. As I worked with her we tried to maintain focus and make sure that what she was doing within her school and with her staff aligned to her goals and vision, which they did. The issue was that some of the adults on the campus lost sight of the concept of making decisions based on the students, not the adults in the building. On one particular day towards the end of her first year, my phone rang and as I picked up I could hear the frustration in her voice. The principal was upset, frustrated, and tired. She had been losing sleep thinking about all the different things that needed to be changed and was afraid that progress wasn't happening. I asked the same question that I ask many educators, "How do you maintain motivation and a positive attitude?" She paused as every educator does and responded she was too tired to stay motivated. This is the issue that haunts so many of educators. Our hearts and souls are poured into our work each and every day and when it comes down to staying motivated and being intentional we are tired. As educators, we have a duty to look out for each other and share with one another how we stay positive and motivated. This is something that unfortunately is not covered in principal school, but without it the numbers of our principals that experience a lack of motivation will skyrocket.

Growing up I never considered myself a writer. Of course, I would write papers for school and whenever I needed. As some of my peers would struggle through writing, I seemed to be able to get things down on paper and move on. Throughout high school, I wasn't the best reader, but my writing pulled me through. The same continued for me throughout college. As I became a teacher I found myself extremely motivated at the beginning. As the years went by the motivation and positivity would fluctuate. This hurt not only myself, but it affected my students. Something needed to change. I began looking for something to pick me up. I would get professional magazines sent to my school on a regular basis and decided that I had something to offer as well. I started writing articles about teaching and how educators could make a difference. Suddenly my articles were getting published and my motivation increased drastically. This has led me to writing as a reflection tool that I took and slightly changed to help me figure out why I became a school leader.

Becoming a school leader adds a new dynamic in any educator's life. The stress, responsibility, and demands of the job are enough to rock anyone at the beginning of the journey. I no longer had time to write articles for publication, nor did I have time to read those articles about the profession and soon I felt the effects of stress and had symptoms of burnout. Knowing that something needed to change I took the advice of members of my Principals In Action PLN and started a blog. At first, I hesitated as I thought who would want to read a blog about things happening to me in my professional and personal life. I thought to myself that I had a fairly large family, so maybe 50-75 people would read my posts, but that was it. As soon as I started to write I could feel the energy that I sparked within myself and the drive to do things differently reemerged. I hit submit and soon after people started reading and responding. A few days later I posted another blog and more readers joined in. Some of my staff would read and this allowed for dialogue and understanding of what was happening and how everyone fits in the puzzle to change and make things better. I continued to write often and purposefully. The blog was just an avenue and I wrote for myself, but soon my writing was helping others and that put a fire in me even more. I was hooked. I continue to write and reflect and encourage everyone to find something that motivates you and make you want to become better.

Sometimes the motivation comes from working closely with staff and students. Jay has made it a priority to meet with grade level teams of teachers on a weekly basis with an agenda that always starts with kids. Maintaining the focus on the kids is what is motivating for Jay. Being in classrooms to watch our students and staff in action is what gets Jay refocused and provides the impetus to be better today than he was yesterday. After all, if we compare ourselves to others, we'll always fall short. If we just try to be better today than we were yesterday, that's the only true measure of improvement.

To stay motivated, Mark has found that it's important to remember and reflect on his "Why." Recently, Mark shared with other elementary principals and his staff, "Why I Am a Champion of the Underdog." Mark talked about the challenges he faced growing up, most of which staff at school had no idea he was experiencing. It was because of teachers, counselors and a high school principal that Mark felt safe and supported. It was because of those educators in Mark's early life, that he stays motivated to be a champion for the underdog. We all have students who are going things we're aware of, and many that we don't know about, and we can be their champions through our presence, words, and actions, and you can't do that by staying in your office.

Every person is different when it comes to motivation. You must continue to seek what actually motivates you and how you can find it when you actually need it.

The Value of Being a Connected Educator
Ellen O'Neill Elementary Principal, Southold, NY

It is an honor to be the lead learner at Southold Elementary School. I GET to spend my days surrounded by the most amazing kids and a talented, dedicated staff. What could be better? But, being a principal doesn't guarantee that you are a Principal In Action. It is a conscious choice we need to make to ensure that as the lead learner, we spend the majority of our time out of the office and with kids. Be it arrival in the morning, the cafeteria during lunch, the playground during recess, classrooms during instruction, or dismissal in the afternoon, I prefer to be out and about, rather than in my office.

I have grown as a leader over the years and need to give credit to the members of my PLN. Being a connected educator has opened up my circle and ensured that I continually learn from like-minded edus. I have friends across the country that I've never met in person, but I feel like I've known them all my life. Using Voxer, Twitter, Instagram and Facebook allows me to interact with some rock star principals (and other educators) on a daily basis. I constantly talk about "My principal friend from Texas/Wisconsin/Kansas/ North Carolina/Massachusetts, etc. who said..." We learn from each other, share our struggles and successes, and support each other through the daily life of being a principal. I am a better principal/lead learner because of each and every one of them. Thanks PIA (Principals In Action) and MAPS (#momsasprincipals) friends!

We all know that there will be managerial tasks or situations that arise which prevent us from being a principal in action at times. When I began as a principal 14 years ago, I allowed those situations to take more of my time than I do now. I've learned to better prioritize and to know that we will never actually be caught up or done. It is still difficult at times, but my PLN helps keep me on track and reminds me that even on those days, we need to make time to be with kids. Plus, it's those hugs, fist bumps, and high fives that make the tough days better.

There are so many wonderful things happening around Southold Elementary School everyday and I don't want to miss any of it. I have found that the best way to showcase the amazingness is through social media. Instagram, Facebook and Twitter tell our story. Many of the staff members have Twitter accounts and they use them to share our story, as well. It's a positive and timely way to let the families and community know what's going on at SES.

Challenge

Think about how you stay motivated. Share this technique with your staff and with others and, when talking to others, ask them how they stay motivated and share your tips. Think about a world where everyone stays positive and motivated. That would be a world where I would want my kids to be.

Chapter 13

Dealing with Behavior

(Ryan Sheehy)

Behavior is inevitably part of every school. It is something that happens on the bus, in the classroom, on the playground, in the cafeteria, in the quad and is a constant wherever you go. The behavior can be positive or negative in nature but it is still there. Since the behavior is inevitable, the only option that we have is how we react to it. The reaction that we give to any certain situation sets the tone for every interaction that you have with that student again.

There are many different behaviors that you may see in education. There are differences between elementary and high school students, but they all have a common theme. The common theme that they all have is that they are attention seeking. They may be peer attention seeking, while others may be adult attention seeking.

While I was visiting another school doing instructional

rounds, the principal got a support call into a fourth grade classroom. While walking with the principal to the classroom, the principal told me all about the student and how many times he gets called into the classroom for support with this particular student. As we entered the classroom, all but this one student were transitioning out of this classroom going to the science lab. The principal, myself, and this student were the only ones that remained in this room. The student refused to look at anyone and just put his head down, while not talking at all. The principal continued to try and talk with him, but in reality, it was just him talking at him. I looked at him and asked him if he worked out. The student looked up and I told him that I love doing push-ups with students. I dropped right there and did 10 push-ups. He gave me that look that meant he thought I was a little crazy but he was intrigued. After I was done with the push-ups, I asked him if he could do any. He dropped down right there and did 10. I looked at the principal and said your turn. Then we all did 10 more together. I explained to the student that when I am having a hard time, I sometimes do push-ups to refocus and get my energy back. He liked the idea and asked the principal if he could try that. The principal agreed and for the rest of the year when he needed a break, he would come to the office and do some push-ups. The technique was designed to give the student a break and an opportunity to release endorphins and change the behavior before it happens, while teaching them a self-regulation tactic.

When I arrived at the elementary school after being appointed principal, there was a student who had been a high flyer in the office. He was being sent to the office for multiple reasons and he would be sent multiple times a week. There was no one constant behavior or precedent that anyone was able to figure out. I tried connecting with him, I tried building a relationship. He didn't want anything to do with me and this continued for the first year of me leading the school. As year two started I thought that I would try to build upon the relationship and change his perception of the principal, but had my work cut out for me. As I tried to change the perception it was continued to be met with resistance and it quickly became evident that it was going to be an uphill battle. I decided to back off and deal with behaviors and interactions from a different perspective. Using current teacher and past teachers, the student interactions were handled in a different way and with the use of teacher check in. Understanding that every student will not mesh with you is key and making sure that they get the support that is needed.

Behavior can take all your time as a leader and can make for some long days. When you go home at night most likely it will occupy your mind and you will be thinking about how you might be able to change the relationship in the future. Students will remember the way you treated them more than they will remember what you taught them.

Mark has discovered that by being a principal in action, he is able to stay connected with students who may have a higher likelihood of needing to take time out of class or be referred to the office for support. By being visible and present in classrooms, hallways, the playground, and in the cafeteria, Mark has been able to establish and develop relationships with students. He has been able to check in with them during their learning, has watched their interactions with peers outside, and has provided proactive breaks and connection time.

Some of these connections are done by spending one-on-one time with specific students in Mark's office talking, problem-solving, reading, coding, programming, creating, and learning. By being a principal in action, you are able to be out of your office and see how students are behaving, performing, and engaging throughout their day. As a principal in action, you also need to make sure there are support and communication systems in place when you are needed. Mark's support team includes the school counselor and a student support specialist. Mark works to communicate with the office team when he is out and about in the building, visiting classrooms, reading to classes, supervising on the playground, conducting formative observations, or participating in activities. Mark responds to an email message (low level), text messages (mid-level), or phone calls, walkie-talkie calls, or all-school announcements (highest level) when he is out of his office and not easily accessible.

Working in a middle school provides different behavioral challenges for Jay. Students can be bigger, louder, and stronger so finding ways to develop relationships becomes a little trickier. Jay has found ways that allow him to check in with students. By being at the student drop off and walking the hallways in the morning, Jay is able to get a pulse of the school right away. He remembers conversations he has had with students earlier in the week and finds ways to check in while in the hallway, in classrooms, at lunch, and at recess. Taking students on a "walk and talk" is often much better than having a conversation in his office. It's not that an office conversation isn't necessary, there are always times to have those sorts of conversations, but not every conversation about behavior needs to happen in the office.

Jay has also realized that his relationships with students are not the same as the teachers' relationships with the students. Sometimes Jay will cover a class for a while so that the teacher can deal with the behavior. Ultimately, the relationship the teacher has with the student is much more important than the relationship between the principal and the student. The teacher should be spending more time with the student than the principal does. If that isn't the case, then something else needs to be done. Jay works with the teachers to come up with a plan to help create and foster and build the relationships so that they become so strong that the students want to behave in order to stay in class.

Good and bad behavior is not going anywhere. Leaders are and will be faced with it forever, but how you respond to it is up to you. Relationships, relationships, and relationships are three words that can change everything. Working on those while dealing with behavior is a game changer.

Challenge

Look around your school/classroom and find the student that stands out to you. Sit down with them at lunch for a few days and build a relationship by discussing something that they love to do. Then make a plan to do that activity with them. Write about your experience and share with others the power that having a conversation has.

Chapter 14

How Will You Be Remembered?

(Ryan Sheehy)

When America thinks about principals they tend to think about principals that they either had in school or the ones portrayed in Hollywood. Mr. Belding (Saved By The Bell), Mr. Feeny (Boy Meets World), Mr. Rooney (Ferris Bueller's Day Off), and Mr. Strickland (Back To The Future) are a few that come to mind. These principals stand out in people's minds because they were part of television history and they have depicted education in a comedic way. How will you be remembered by teachers, students, parents and the community?

That question is one that I often reflect on and think that every educator, professional, and human being should think about. At the end of our life our money, possessions, fame, whatever else you may consider will not matter. All that you will leave behind is your legacy. When it comes down to it, how you treat others and your impact on the world is what defines you.

As a first year teacher, I listened to others telling me that you shouldn't smile for the first few months and you needed to be strict out of the gate and lay down the law. I understood what others were trying to share with me, but I also understood that those students would remember me, but why? They would remember those characteristics about me. They remember how I treated them way before they would remember what I taught them. Unfortunately, I learned the hard way from the first few years of teaching. Reflection from years later showed me that I could have been much better in my early years, but since that was in the past I had to learn from it and move forward. As a leader, I try to make sure that I am positively impacting someone's life each day and that can be accomplished in so many different ways. Now one of my goals with every student that I encounter is that I will be someone that they tell their grandchildren about. I want to make that kind of impact.

When Mark thinks back to his elementary, middle, and high school years, he remembers things that had an impact on him. A field trip to Hartwick Pines State Park, being in the cast of school plays, and an English Literature teacher who gave students choices in how to demonstrate their learning. Mark tries to carry those memories with him in his role as principal. He wants students to remember him for the time he brought them to his office and they called the student's parents with the #GoodNewsCallOfTheDay. He wants students to remember the time he was slimed wearing his suit and tie to pay up for students meeting a community goal. He also wants students to remember him for sitting down next to them during a lesson and having the student explain what they were working on.

Creating a legacy and memorable moments won't happen sitting in your office. Get out, be among students, have fun with them, attend their games and performances, do things that will have them remembering you.

Jay does his best to connect with students by being an active participant in classes, playing at recess, and sitting down with students during lunch. One other thing that Jay really enjoys are monthly assemblies. Ten years ago, in order to find a way to provide more time for professional development and collaboration time for our teachers, the two principals in our district agreed to do a monthly assembly for 30 minutes to start the school day. These allowed for two things- time for teachers and a chance for the principals to connect with the students in a different way- while not changing the student drop off time. Does this have you intrigued and wondering how this happens? Are you thinking about how you can do this in your school? Here is the plan Jay uses.

The assemblies take place in the gym as there is no auditorium in Jay's school. The first assemblies Jay used a portable projector and a pull-down screen while the students sat in the bleachers. Now there is an electric powered screen and a fixed projector that can be used by our PE classes and for other assemblies and celebrations. Backpacks are set on the floor around the perimeter of the gym in spots designated by the homeroom teacher's name. Students sit in the bleachers in spots designated by the homeroom teacher's name. The only other adults in the gym are instructional assistants that are assigned to specific students. Otherwise, it's Jay in the gym with 400+ students. That's the easy part. The more difficult part is putting together the message for the students.

Most of Jay's messages have to do with Merton's three rules- Be kind, be safe, and do your job. Students are greeted by a song and once the song has ended, we say the pledge, Jay does the announcements and celebrates students, and then the presentation begins. Jay includes quotes, videos, and his own personal stories, and occasionally tears are shed by Jay, the students, and the teachers (Sometimes the teachers sneak in to see the final video as it can provide a great conversation starter in homeroom.). This has helped Jay to be seen by the students in a different way and allows them to know Jay better. This is how relationships start and build. The students see Jay in a way that makes him more personable and relatable. Often, the students talk about the videos and stories that Jay has shared when they see him in the school or when they return to visit.

Student Connections: Make Them Often & Strong as the Head Learner

Mike Budisch, retiring Primary School Principal from Merton, WI

You may wonder about the title of this section, and where did the "Head Learner" title originate. I'll get to that later, right now is the time for you to imagine school days that are driven by one caveat-how do I connect with the kids today. Some days are driven by a more precise purpose with a check in with some of my "closest friends". Many days are focused on the larger vision of grade levels, or specific classrooms, and others by assessing the culture of our school. Still, our bottom line as a school, and mine as the Head Learner is to nurture and focus on our children's growth. To ensure that, children need to believe that you believe in them and their potential. As you continue to read on, consider your collective conversations over the course of the day. Are there more conversations with the children? Or, are there more conversations with adults?

As the day begins, early, with the rigors of the emails, and unlocking classrooms, attendance at IEPs, I anticipate the greetings of the children each morning on the playground where we meet before school. This is where the happenings of the night before or the past weekend are regaled in full with tales of accomplishments and visits to far off locations, like grandmas and grandpas. I learn of the newly lost teeth, the new pair of shoes, sleepovers, and what was eaten for breakfast. Some may call this minutiae that doesn't need the light of day, yet to our youngsters, the opportunity to share their lives is invaluable. As their principal, the story of their lives unfold before me, and I can revel with them as I ask the questions that reveal their young and emerging values-what is truly important to them, in that very moment.

Ah, the moments, how do we make sure these happen? How can we ensure that, that one moment isn't missed? We should make the time to develop and build upon the connections, the most valuable part of our days. Examples include the moments we are cruising the halls, you know what I mean, when the classes are passing. We notice the art smocks on the 5K and first graders that once belonged to their dad-old golf shirts, T-shirts, and the dress shirts that all touch the floor.

Each day, I find examples of the fun times on the playground where I push the swings-"Just one more time Mr. B!" Or "Watch me on the bar Mr. B, watch what I can do!" or "Are you going to play 4-square with us Mr. B? Oh no…." I find myself in such an enjoyable place with them. It also provides me with opportunities to de-escalate issues that always seem to arise at the close of recess. The winners and losers somehow find themselves right next to each other in line, and I can play the diplomat to help settle the issue.

Sitting down at a table full of 5Kers who are eating their lunches makes my day. I learn about their favorite foods, what they don't like, and presents from birthdays or holidays. They enjoy watching me eat and ask those

> precious questions that always start with "Why?" These moments slow my day down to realize the children are what makes me tick, not the curriculum or department meeting at the close of the day.
>
> I have learned from my connections and moments with children, and how this has contributed to my evolution as the Head Learner. Be the one who connects with them.

Educators work hard each and every day to make an impact on the students that they have. Leaders do the same thing and try to make an impact on those that they lead. When we retire or pass on all we are left with is the memory of what we have done. This is your legacy. What will be your legacy? What will your students be telling their grandchildren about you?

Challenge

Reflect on how students, parents, teachers, and community members will remember you. What can you do to impact someone's life positively every day and share that with others around you?

Chapter 15

It's Not Just About the Kids

(Jay Posick)

Recently I was asked to share ways that I encourage our teachers to be amazing. I was asked to share specific examples of feedback I had provided as well as if it was impactful and/or implemented by the teacher. I reflected on this request and came up with the following list.

Classroom Visits

I visit classrooms every day. Although it's powerful to visit classrooms to connect with students, it's also powerful to visit classrooms to see staff work their magic in their rooms. Occasionally staff will ask me why I haven't visited in a while because I am in classrooms so often. I use a Google sheet to keep track of visits and the type of feedback I provided. Classroom visits are one of the impactful practices that any leader can do. Getting into the classrooms shows leadership what is happening on the ground floor. Too often decisions are made from the top, without truly knowing what is happening in the classroom and at our schools. The visits need to be purposeful and impactful. Too often we get into a place where we are being pulled in so many ways and forget to make sure that our visits are driving instruction.

Following almost every classroom visit, I do one of the following things. I make eye contact, give a thumbs up, fist bump or high five, or share a comment. These are not formal bits of feedback, but they are feedback that teachers come to enjoy and expect.

Ryan also makes it a point to use visual cues when visiting a classroom. He wants teachers to make sure that they feel supported and that he is only a phone call away at a moments notice if something comes up or is needed.

Face to Face Conversations

These are the best ways of getting to know your staff. It's a time to put down your phone or laptop and pay attention to what's being said. These conversations can occur during prep time, before or after school, during lunch time, and at passing time. I just recently had my favorite conversations with staff as we spent 15 minutes for a "halftime" talk, discussing what they wanted to celebrate from the first semester, what they were proud of from the first semester, and how I can better support them so that their second semester is as good as, if not better, than their first semester.

When Ryan was named principal for the first time at an elementary school and he made a point that he valued face to face conversations. Before the school year started, Ryan set up meetings offsite at a coffee shop with every single member of his staff. The conversation was not centered around school, but more centered around people and things that they wanted or needed. It gave Ryan insight and much needed relationships before the school year started.

Handwritten Notes

Who doesn't like a handwritten note? I don't do this often enough, but when I do, I know that it makes a big impact. I also share handwritten holiday cards right before Winter Break. I have stopped in classrooms days, weeks, months, and years later, and I see some of them posted on file cabinets or on walls. I actually have a file folder of notes that I've received that I look through whenever I need a pick me up.

Ryan loves getting handwritten notes in the mail and has used that practice with staff and students. Every year in the month of December, Ryan and his staff take time to write cards for students. Then sometime over the course of winter break, those cards are mailed home. The feedback from families has been incredible. Ryan saw the impact that handwritten notes had on students and their families. He decided that the same thing needed to happen with his staff. Since handwriting notes occasionally, Ryan has seen other educators follow suit and write their colleagues notes and cards.

Voxer Messages

One of my favorite apps is Voxer. From time to time I'll use the "My Notes" feature in Voxer to record a message after I've been in a class. Then, while I'm walking to the next classroom, I'll send the voxer message via email to the teacher.

Voxer has been a game changer for teacher feedback for

Ryan. He is able to keep up his busy pace all day long, because he can leave quick practical feedback and move onto the next classroom. Teachers then can respond to the feedback and keep the dialogue and guided practice going for days to come. Makes the initial classroom visit much more impactful.

Student Learning Objective/ Professional Practice Goals Meetings

These SLO/PPG meetings are part of the evaluation process for all teachers in our district. The teacher and I collaborate to determine the objectives and goals to start the year. We then meet halfway through the year to celebrate and adjust the objectives and goals. At the end of the year, we meet one final time to celebrate the progress of our students.

These meetings give Ryan an opportunity to coach and create goals alongside teachers making sure that the goals align with that year's school goals. When everyone is working towards the same goals, it makes the learning more relevant for all, since it doesn't feel that everyone is going in different directions, which will then lead to more buy-in from staff members.

Pre-Observation/ Post-Observation Meetings

These meetings are part of the formal evaluation process with teachers on cycle. There is a formal written part by the teacher for the pre-observation meeting. We meet to discuss what the teacher wants me to look for during the observation. I take notes during the observation and then tag these notes as evidence, which I share with the teacher. We finish up this process by both filling out our own post-observation reflection. We exchange and read our reflections, and then the magic begins. This is when we get to talk about the celebrations from the lesson as well as any suggestions for improvement moving forward. The paperwork is important, but the conversations are vital.

Ryan uses these observation meetings as a coaching opportunity and an opportunity to dig into content looking for trends across the school and how does it line up to the priorities of the central office when it comes to instruction and content delivery.

Social Media Posts

If something is posted on social media it is part of the story of our school. Some posts are made by me, but others are posted by other staff members. I almost always retweet these posts that our staff shares on social media. We use two hashtags, #mertonint and #MertonProud, when we post on Twitter (@mertonint). Our school Instagram account (mertonint) is followed by many of our students and our school Facebook page (Merton Intermediate School) is followed by many of our families. Posting on social media may not really encourage amazing teachers, but I think if teachers know there is a chance their classroom activities will be posted on social media, they are more apt to want to provide amazing learning opportunities for our students.

In a follow-up conversation with the person asking me about how I encourage teachers to be amazing, I stated this fact (well, it's a fact to me.). Teachers won't be amazing unless they want to be amazing. If a teacher wants to be amazing, then it's possible that a principal, or a colleague, or a friend, or a family member can encourage them to be even more amazing. Hopefully, the ideas I mentioned in this post have helped me encourage our teachers to be even more amazing then they thought they could be.

Ryan visits classrooms to visit with students and showcase the work that is happening inside the rooms. There are so many amazing things happening and often get overlooked because no one outside of the teachers and students sees it. Ryan feels that it is an important piece to look at while making visits to our classrooms.

Recently, Mark was communicating with one of the special education paraprofessionals who was questioning her worth and value because no one shows her appreciation. This affected Mark and made him remember how important it is to reach out, provide feedback, give affirmation, express appreciation, and show all employees that they are valued and important. This might be easier to do with staff members during a formal observation, but you need to find ways to reach out, connect with, support, provide feedback, and show appreciation to all staff members. That includes not just classroom teachers, but other licensed staff members, paraprofessionals, clerical staff, custodians, food service members, and bus drivers. Leaders need to find ways to connect with all employees.

Challenge

Use the suggestions from this chapter and provide feedback to a staff member or staff members. Try to get to each staff member this month and see if it makes a difference in the culture and climate in the school.

Chapter 16

Breaking Down Barriers

(Jay Posick)

Get Out of Your Office.

Five words that should be so easy to accomplish, but we all know that there are times when it just can't be done. Sometimes it's the unexpected meetings or discipline issues. Sometimes it's the paperwork. Sometimes it's an expectation of the district office. Whatever the situation, sometimes there are barriers that prevent us from being out of our offices and in classrooms and other environments in our schools.

When I was a first year principal, I wanted to be in as many classrooms as I could. I was not only a first year principal, but I was in a new school and district so not many people knew me. This was in 2007, well before the world and schools are as connected as they are now. Whenever I walked into classrooms that first month of school, instruction stopped and the staff and students all said, "Hello, Mr. Posick." Some staff even asked if I needed a student, or them, for a discussion. That was the way the previous principal did things. He mostly visited to find a student, a staff member, or for a formal observation. That wasn't the only time he visited, but based upon my first month, it sure seemed that way.

I'm not a big fan of staff meetings. I have weekly grade level meetings where I am able to provide the same information to all staff in smaller environments, which also leads to potentially deeper conversations. After my first month of school, however, I decided I needed to call an all staff meeting. The topic was this- classroom visits. I assured the staff that my visits were meant to allow me to learn about the culture of each classroom as well as to learn about the students and how they were learning. These visits weren't evaluative, they were fact-finding missions. I wanted to see the students and teachers in action. Most of the staff realized the purpose and just kept right on facilitating learning, which was what I wanted them to do. I wanted to create a school culture that wasn't built on "gotcha" but instead built on "gotcha back".

Twelve years later, I have a spreadsheet I use to keep track of classroom visits and types of feedback given (note, vox, walkthrough, observation). If I notice I haven't visited a classroom for a day or two, then I make sure to visit the following day. It's also important to note that the teachers know when I haven't visited for a while. They either email me or find me in the hallway and ask if they've done something wrong. And that's a good thing. If you build a school culture that expects the principal to visit classrooms, that's good for everyone.

One of the barriers Mark has needed to overcome are the perceptions others have for the principal. Not everyone sees the same value for being out of the office or developing relationships with students. On a recent survey Mark administered to staff members, one question asked, "Am I accessible to you?" One staff member's response was, "Yes, but only when you are finished on the playground or are done reading to classes." Mark viewed this response that people were noticing he wanted to be out of his office building relationships and connecting with others. Mark also realized he needed to communicate strategies on how to reach him via walkie talkie, text message, phone, or email message with questions and concerns when he was not in his office. Staff members want their principal to be visible, connecting, engaging, visiting, and supporting, but they also were to know how to connect and get ahold of the principal when needed.

Ryan believes that all of the strategies above are important but should become a natural part of the position. The role of the leader is constantly changing and how those leaders handle the job, must as well. When I told Ryan the story of my friend that blind casts over his shoulder, Ryan said he was just trying something different, hoping to get a different result. Don't be afraid of trying new things. Don't be afraid to cast over your shoulder every once and awhile. Taking those risks will lead to breaking down barriers that are important in any leadership position, no matter if it is in a school, business, or the classroom.

I like to fish, and often I'm fishing with my friends or family. A friend of mine who I fished with regularly used to say, "Expect the unexpected" whenever we were fishing and not catching anything. He would toss the bait or lure back over his shoulder, a blind cast hoping to find that one lone fish that would turn our luck. That might work for fishing, but it certainly doesn't work for school leadership. If we do something by chance, you never know what you might find. That friend of mine I fish with, he rarely if ever caught anything with his blind casts. If we do something by chance as a school leader, the only thing we might catch is a situation we wouldn't want. So what can we do to handle these barriers and get into more classrooms? Here are some ideas.

Take Control of Your Calendar

Although I have a lot of open spots on my calendar, there are many spots that are always filled. Lunch and recess duty is a daily occurrence for me. I seldom have meetings scheduled during our lunch and recess times. If I need to meet with someone during lunch, I find someone to cover for me and provide them a GOOSE (Get Out Of School Early) pass to be used at a time that works for both of us. I have grade level meetings every Thursday that rarely if ever get rescheduled. My secretary has control of my calendar and my routine and often runs interference so that I can stay out of my office as long as possible each day. One great thing about being a principal is the flexibility of your calendar. It can also be a not so great thing. If you take control of your calendar, you have the opportunity to decide when you have meetings and how long those meetings will last.

Alternate Times and Locations to Complete Paperwork

All educators have to handle paperwork, or computer work, as part of their job. When do you get your paperwork done? Does it have to be done in your office? Does it have to be done when staff and students are in the building? I like to get my paperwork done in my office, but only when students and staff aren't in school. It may happen before the school day begins or after it's over. Sometimes I might even come into school on the weekends. We all know that some of our work as an educator can happen at any time. The key is to make sure that when you come in early or stay late or come in over the weekend that you focus your time on that paperwork.

I also do some of my paperwork in classrooms while teachers are facilitating learning and our learners are learning. I'm in classrooms so often that teachers and students alike don't really know the reason for my visit. That may sound strange, but I could be doing an observation or answering emails or finding a student I need to speak with or writing a blog or learning with the students. Or I could be doing paperwork. If you are in classes enough, you can do paperwork in classrooms. No one would know, except maybe you. The benefit of being in classrooms, even if you're doing "principal work" is that you know what's happening. There are fewer surprises. But let's face it, students and staff alike behave differently in class when the principal is there. However, the more you're in classrooms the more genuine the learning and behavior will be. If you're in classrooms enough, there won't be as big a divide in learning or behavior from when you are in the classroom and when you aren't in the classroom. The expectation is that students and staff won't know when you'll stop in, so the more likely they are at or close to their "A game" all the time.

Be Thoughtful Scheduling Meetings
As principals, we have lots of meetings that we need to

attend. Some we call (staff meetings, grade level meetings, building leadership team meetings, family meetings, individual meetings with staff or students) while we are called to others (administrative meetings, board meetings, curriculum meetings, teacher negotiations). Meetings are a necessary evil but if they are scheduled outside of normal school learning hours, you can still be in classrooms and other spaces during the day. Some meetings need to be scheduled during the school day so, if possible, pick a day that's going to be your meeting day. I (Jay) have all of my grade level meetings on Thursdays, and everyone knows it. My secretary often tries to plan family meetings or school tours on Thursdays so that only one day of the week is impacted by meetings. It doesn't always happen, but it's something that she and I try to make happen.

Challenge

Identify one barrier that is keeping you from being out of your office more and use one of the suggested strategies to overcome that barrier. Make the strategy a habit and show others that by creating the habit, it allows for much personal growth and will help others see it from a different perspective.

Chapter 17

Formal Observations and Feedback

(Jay Posick)

One of my favorite things to do is be in classrooms. Sometimes I'm in classrooms to watch the teacher, sometimes to watch the kids, and sometimes to get in the middle of it all and learn with the kids. I visit enough classrooms every day that occasionally the teachers and students don't even know that I stopped in. I think that's a good thing because I get to see what's organically happening in classrooms. There's no way to put on a "dog and pony show" if you don't know when the principal is going to stop into your classroom. I think because of these visits, the actual formal observation part of the evaluation is less frightening for our teachers. They do what they do every day because it's what is best for kids. They invite me in when they are trying something new in their classes, either to show me because they are excited or because they would like some honest feedback.

When teachers want to take a risk and they invite you in to

see it, that's some pretty awesome stuff. Being a principal in action who is out of his office allows me to really know what's going on in our school, but it's also important to provide feedback to our staff.

Ryan uses very similar ways to make sure that the feedback that is needed is happening. When Ryan talks about needing feedback, he is very serious. Without intentional feedback, we do not see the growth needed and desired by professionals and students. Ryan looks at his own professional journey and the feedback that has been delivered to him over the years. Too often the feedback comes in short bursts, only around the evaluation season. Ryan craves feedback and purposeful feedback that will help him grow as an educator and a person. Leaders that provide true feedback will see the benefits spread across their organization. Be intentional and honest.

One of the barriers that Ryan is often confronted with is the barrier of time. Everyone faces this barrier and it comes down to priorities and skills of time management. Ryan has created different observation tools that help make sure the feedback is timely and provides data that drives conversation in the classroom. While also using the strategies that I mentioned above, Ryan has a Google form that tracks classroom observation and data, while also sending it immediately to the teacher when he walks out of the room.

Mark observes probationary teachers three times a year and one-third of the tenured staff once a year. Not every standard can be observed during one specific lesson. By being out of your office visiting classrooms regularly, you have so many more opportunities to observe and provide feedback to teachers. One of the domains of the formative observation form Mark uses with his teachers is "Professionalism." By being out of the office and seeing teachers in a variety of settings, Mark gains a broader perspective of how they are growing and developing professionally, collaborating with colleagues, and communicating with others, all standards under the Professionalism domain.

Challenge

Make a plan to provide feedback to each of your teaching staff this month. The feedback does not need to be with your school or district's formal evaluation documents, but it still should be meaningful. If you have an assistant principal, include them in the challenge, too.

Chapter 18

Thanking and Appreciating Staff

(Jay Posick)

I heard from my superintendent that it takes $600 to motivate someone to do something. I don't know about you, but I don't have $600 in my school or personal budget for one, let alone all, of our school staff. I would also tell you that it doesn't take money to show thanks or appreciation. It just takes the ability to care and encourage with words, deeds, food, and an occasional dress up day. It is also, in my opinion, more appreciated when it is unexpected. There are times that are perfect for showing thanks and appreciation (staff appreciation week, before holiday breaks, at the end of the school year) but there are also other times when we should show thanks and appreciation.

Imagine showing up after a snow or cold day (I live in Wisconsin) to find a soup lunch provided by the building leadership team. How about a jeans day after four straight five day weeks? On a bone chilling-day, it's time for a sweatshirt or sweater day. These are just some ideas. Many more have been shared on the #principalsinaction hashtag on Twitter. My favorite idea, however, is one that just blew away our staff.

The administrative team at our school wanted to surprise staff and show them that they are appreciated. Custodians, instructional assistants, teachers, and office staff were all celebrated. There was nothing special about the selected day at all. It was randomly chosen. The planning was as stealthy as I have ever seen. We involved our PTO to get volunteers for all of our classroom teachers as well as our cafeteria supervisors. Only a few adults (secretaries, nurse, one on one instructional assistants) were left behind, and our superintendent spoke to each of them about the reasons why they were staying behind. These staff members received separate recognition and lunch on the district at another time. We had parent volunteers meet in the cafeteria to receive their assignments for classroom coverage. They were all nervously excited. At 11:25 I sent them on their way. At 11:30, with a volunteer standing at the doors of each classroom, I got on the PA and told all staff to come to the lobby, with their coat and without their lunch. The volunteers were there to cover for them.

The staff arrived in the lobby and waited for directions from me. Some staff had out their phones for pictures or video as none of them knew what was going on. Some even thought they were in trouble. Once the staff was all gathered, I told them that they were to get on the school bus parked out front. They were going out to lunch, on the district, and would be brought back to school at 1:00. They were taken to our local golf course where a catered meal awaited them. This was the epitome of a duty-free lunch. The volunteers and the essential staff that was left back at the schools covered classes, lunch duty, and recess duty, and they did an amazing job. The coolest part was the discussions I had with the students about what the teachers were doing. They thought it was amazing, and they behaved better for the volunteers than we could have hoped. It's not something that we will be able to pull off again, but it was definitely a day that none of our staff will forget. And those staff who were asked to stay behind got gift cards in appreciation of needing to stay back with our students and volunteers.

There are also those expected times for thanking and appreciating staff. Staff Appreciation Week is an opportunity for administrators to show their appreciation. If you have a PTO like we do, they can be a partner for funding and ideas. We have had personalized garden rocks to personalized baseball jerseys. These ideas came from our PTO and they develop a theme for the entire week. It may be a bit of a change to our daily schedule, but it's worth it to show thanks and appreciation. I also like to celebrate the "12 Days Before Winter Break" with our staff. There were dress up days, candy, a lunch prepared for the staff by my wife (staff favorite of the celebration), and a final day raffle. Staff enter tickets (received for participating in dress up days) in a basket corresponding to the prize they would like to win. There were gift cards, presentation remotes, kindles, echo dots, and GOOSE (Get Out Of School Early) passes. The prizes were delivered by our school mascot (me) who happens to be wearing a Santa jacket and hat. It's a great end to the final day before Winter Break, and the culmination of showing thanks and appreciation to all of our staff.

Throughout Mark's administrative career, he has tried different strategies and techniques for recognizing staff members, some with more success than others. Mark has had a belief that all staff members (licensed, non-licensed, clerical, food service, custodial, bus drivers) should receive thanks and appreciation. More often Mark tries to do school-wide recognitions that include starting the day with coffee and donuts, hosting a mid-winter meltdown with Hawaiian pizza and smoothies, or preparing lunch or dinner during conferences. In one of his schools, Mark implemented the Roving Roadrunner Award with the goal of passing the Roving Roadrunner Award weekly to a new deserving staff member. On Monday, Mark would deliver the award to the winner and share why they were receiving the award. He would pick it up on Friday to share with another staff member the next week. This worked for a year and it was powerful for Mark to give the award directly to a colleague explaining the reasons for that. During the second year of this award, the weekly winner would present it to someone else the following week, and so on for the year. The Roving Roadrunner Award was accompanied by a staff roster so staff could see who hadn't received it yet and share it with someone accordingly. This was a good way to have a strategy where colleagues could recognize colleagues.

It's All About Relationships

Bobbie French, Elementary Principal, Phillipston, MA

It's all about relationships. I work hard to develop positive and trusting relationships with students and staff. Smiles, high fives and fist bumps go a long way but I love showing my teachers and staff a little more appreciation.

They work so hard for all of our children and I want them to know their efforts are recognized and appreciated. I have started doing simple things like leaving them "You Rock" postcards complete with Bitmoji and chocolates or Anchors of Appreciation postcards letting them know what I noticed while visiting their classrooms. Scratch off turkeys, elves or pots of gold are fun anytime of the year. The favorite scratch-off prize - a jeans day. Another simple thing we can do that means so much to our staff.

I also love doing many of the other appreciation days like "Orange You Glad..." and filling the staff lounge will all orange treats. In the winter a favorite is the "Hot Cocoa Bar" complete with all the fixings including Fluff (It's a New England thing) or a "Popcorn Bar" with lots of mix-ins to choose from. Teachers know you're thinking of them when you take the time to set up something special just for them. It's not about how cute it all looks, although that helps, but that you went out of your way to do something kind and appreciative.

I filled the staff fridge with orange and grape "Crush" after we crushed the first trimester. It's the unexpectedness of some of these little things that have the most impact. I always love hearing how much staff enjoy these treats and hope they know how much I appreciate all that they do. A new tradition before Christmas break is the 10 days before Christmas Break where I do something special each day. We have book swaps, crazy sweater days, and make Christmas cards for one another. This year we even got a prize wheel and each staff member got to spin the wheel to earn a prize. The students were just as excited watching the teachers as the teachers were to spin the wheel. I've done Fabulous Fridays in February or Marvelous Mondays to get us through those gray, low energy months. Sometimes I break out the Woot Woot Wagon complete with music and snacks on any random day or we do Room Service where the staff get to fill out their room service slip and place it on their doors for an afternoon treat.

No matter what you choose to do, I encourage you to think of something you can do today to show your staff that you appreciate them.

Leaders should be intentional in the way they appreciate their staff. Ryan has seen negative responses to appreciation that was not done intentional and purposeful. When you work with people that are not used to being appreciated, heads turn when you start to appreciate. Some people are very comfortable with it and some are extremely uncomfortable with being appreciated. You must work on building relationships first and then start to give feedback on what you appreciate about them. Use appreciation that specific to the person allowing that person to feel amazing.

Challenge

What is a creative way or fun activity that you have used to show your appreciation for staff members? Share that on Twitter by using the hashtag #PrincipalsInAction or join the Principals In Action Voxer group and share it with others there.

Chapter 19

Sometimes It Takes Three Wheels

(Ryan Sheehy)

The challenge that was dropped for all principals was to get outside their office and go ride a tricycle with kindergarteners. As leaders, we often get sucked into paperwork, politics, and behavior situations (adults and students).

When I was named principal of an elementary school, I was excited to participate in all these challenges that as a high school leader I didn't feel pertained to me. The first day on the job I was riding extremely small tricycles and riding slides with kids. It was a blast. Over the next few years, I continued to do the same, but the stress of the job would occasionally sneak up on me and I would become overwhelmed. On those days that I would become overwhelmed and stressed, I would retreat to the kindergarten yard to ride trikes and go down the slide. Thinking about how riding the trikes made me feel, I decided that others would enjoy it. Partnering with the adaptive physical education teacher, we purchased an adult sized trike.

When ordering the tricycle we looked for something that looked just like the kind of trikes that our school had and looked like the adults on our campus would enjoy. Weeks later the bike arrived in multiple pieces. It took a few days, but finally, I had the time to assemble it and prepare for the inaugural ride. Prior to its arrival, there were few that knew what would be arriving and those who knew were filled with a childish joy, excited to try it out.

As soon as the tricycle was finished and ready to ride, I rode all over campus and students/adults faces lit up with excitement. I rode around the kindergarten playground and kids wanted to race. I rode around the bigger playground and everyone wanted to take a look. Teachers would come over and ask for a turn. A few weeks had gone by and a teacher came to me extremely upset. There were many things in her life that weren't going well and she needed some help to clear her mind and get motivated again. I told the teacher about some of my "go to" strategies and how those have helped me in times of need. I offered her the opportunity to ride the tricycle. At first, she was apprehensive and thought the idea itself was silly, then she got on. She started to pedal and then she turned around. As she rounded the corner you could see the relief and peace that came across her face. The stress had been reduced and she was having fun. She rode the tricycle all around campus for about 15 minutes. When she got off the bike there was a smile that was glued to her face. She went on to tell others all about her experience.

The next night I had a PTA meeting and came back onto campus around 5:30pm. When I drove up I saw a group of teachers standing in front of the office. They were laughing and having a good time. As I walked towards them I could see what was happening. They were taking turns riding the trike. They were having a blast. Sometimes it takes 3 wheels to put things back into perspective and bring peace into our lives.

Although Jay has ridden a tricycle due to one of the #PrincipalsInAction Twitter challenges, there isn't a tricycle in the school. That doesn't mean that there aren't fun things that the staff and students can participate in. Jay purchased a jammypack, a fanny pack with bluetooth speakers, that he wears for student drop off, lunch and recess, and student pick up. The students and staff can hear him coming because of the music blaring from his jammypack. But Jay isn't the only one who wears the jammypack. At a recent Kindness Olympics Day at school, students were split into teams and needed to come up with a team name and poster that would represent their team. One of the teams asked to borrow my jammypack because they had found a team song. How could Jay say no? The jammypack has become a topic of conversation and always brings a smile to the faces of students and staff. It may not be a tricycle, but it does make everyone feel just a little bit better.

Mark wasn't part of the Principals In Action Voxer group when the Tricycle Challenge was posted. However, he has ridden down the slide, played basketball, jumped rope, weaved in an art class, danced to Go Noodle in classrooms, sang Karaoke during a professional development activity, and had walk-on roles in school musicals. Sometimes it just takes three-wheels or changing your mindset to be a role model and set an example for others.

Leaders are often looked at as uptight and not willing to let loose. It is our job to show them that it is okay to find things that we can enjoy while leading. Look for ways to enjoy the job with students and your staff.

Challenge

What are ways that you can help relieve stress for your students and staff? They don't need to cost money, either. Share your favorite stress relief ideas using the #PrincipalsInAction hashtag.

Chapter 20

Building Staff Relationships

(Ryan Sheehy)

Relationships, Relationships, Relationships. Those three words will change the game at any school in the world. The relationships we form with our students are the foundation that we build academic learning on. Taking that time to build those relationships is vital in the learning of any student and once you build those relationships you will find more time. This is the same with staff members. Too often we forget about the importance of building relationships with every single staff member on our campus.

When I was a physical education teacher at an elementary school, staff relationships were a very important part of our campus. One year a group of teachers met with the principal to discuss how they could boost staff morale and relationships. After that conversation, it was decided that all staff and spouses would be invited to participate in the Amazing Race, Elementary School Style. The teams were picked by a committee in order to be intentional and purposeful with the groupings. The teams were not announced until the night of the event.

On the night of the event, we met at one of our teachers' homes for hors d'oeuvres before we would embark on our fun filled night building relationships and participating in a little friendly competition. Each team was assigned a driver that was not in the competition in order to make sure that all teams followed the traffic laws. Once the first clue was handed out the teams took off. The race took about two hours to complete and had many different stops along the way. Teams had to learn how to Greek dance, find a person in a bar, search a grocery store for a clue, go to the park and go down the slide and many more. The night concluded back at the teacher's house. My team was going fast and strong. Throughout the night it was obvious we were in the lead or real close to the lead. Then suddenly we stopped seeing the team that was neck and neck with us.

When we returned to the house for the finish, the other team we hadn't seen in awhile was sitting there. They claimed to have completed the course ahead of us. It was fun to see the competition not stop, but only get heated up. The teams had to review the evidence and a tiebreaker was decided. Each team was given a tiebreaker song that they had to get up and perform for all the contestants and they would decide the winner. On my team were three teachers, our school counselor and my wife. The song that we were tasked with performing was Ice, Ice, Baby by Vanilla Ice. My wife decided she could rap the whole thing and that we would be the backup dancers and provide the beat. It was absolutely hilarious! The evening brought all the staff together and allowed people to let loose and have fun. We have to take the time to build relationships and not take ourselves too seriously.

Building and facilitating staff relationships is an important part of creating and maintaining a positive school culture and climate and a principal in action can take an active role in helping make that happen. Mark has had conversations with other principals who see themselves as he does, as an extroverted introvert. An extroverted introvert is described as someone who can be charming but also deeply introspective and reflective, someone who needs time to warm up in social situations, and someone who is often confused as an extrovert. We extroverted introverts need to know these things about ourselves so we can plan for and be ready for all of the social situations principals are required to be part of. Mark is making the connection with being an extroverted introvert in this chapter about building staff relationships because it's important to remember that, although your inclination as an extroverted introvert may be to want to connect with a small, select group of individuals, as principal, you need to be developing relationships with all students, families, and staff members. You can use a variety of strategies and methods to do this; one-on-one, in small gatherings, or by being the life of the event.

School Culture is a Tandem Bike, Not a Unicycle

Michael Earnshaw, @mearnshaw158

Relationships first, relationships second, relationships always. This is the mantra I lead by. In order to walk the talk of how important relationships are to the success of a school, leaders need to get out of their office. That's the whole philosophy behind Principals in Action.

Our staff isn't going to know how much we care, more importantly, our students won't know how much we care if we're always in our office behind a desk. We did not become leaders to complete paperwork all day long. We took these positions because we knew we can make more of a difference and improve more lives, both for staff and students! That isn't going to happen stationed behind a desk.

Get out into the halls, into classrooms, talk to people, and get to know their stories. I spend 95% of my day out of my office thanks to my mobile office! If there's something pressing I need to get done, everything is saved on the Cloud and I can work from anywhere on campus. Many times I'll park at a busy intersection in our halls and work. Not only am I productive, but I'm visible and available to everyone. Students will stop and ask how I'm doing or tell me about their weekend and what's going on in their lives. Staff will approach me with issues or questions and we are able to problem solve and collaborate to put out fires before they erupt. We may even pull someone in walking by to get another perspective. I am able to see a student that may need a "pep talk". I'll get down on the ground with them and listen. Being visible and willing to listen shows that we are all in this together!

Establishing a positive, collaborative, and relationship first culture does not just make a school an enjoyable place to go every day, it will inspire, motivate, and push everyone to take risks and be their best. Having the mentality that everyone is in this to help kids succeed and move forward will result in egos being dropped and all staff working together. We have seen more rigor and learning take place with cross curricular lessons that take staff out of their comfort zone. Our school has had students work as teams of surgeons to dissect hearts and then measure their heartbeats. Students needed to rely on each other to solve math puzzles and escape Dr. Doom. I've even got to dance with Cinderella and attend her Royal Ball with our first graders! Not only were these lessons fun for the students, but educational and learning centered. Our Winter Assessment scores showed more growth this year than we've ever experienced!

Every successful school has a positive culture at its forefront. As leaders, we have a strong influence on how our staff, students, and parents play a role in our building's culture. It's imperative that we model what our expectations are for our staff. Time is valuable. How do you spend the little bits of time you have your staff's attention? Are you reading through a PowerPoint? Are you relaying information that can easily be sent out via email? If this is what you're modeling what type of classrooms do you think you're staff will be leading? More than likely your meeting takes place after school, after a long day of teaching. I'm not a betting man, but I would put money down that none of your staff wants to sit for up to two hours listening to you recite bullet points. If we are spending faculty meetings driving data and harping on what isn't working, our staff will in turn always see the negatives in their students and what they're not doing or performing.

On the flipside, if we model risk-taking, getting out of our comfort zones, and building relationships this is what staff will bring to our students. Our staff meetings are conducted in the same manner I would expect to see in our classrooms: collaboration, movement, hands-on, discussions, smiles, and laughter. I like to build anticipation prior to our meetings, giving only a little information to build the excitement of what's to come. Some of our more memorable activities have been Speed Dating, Surviving Struggle Island, and Literature-O-Lanterns. Not only has staff told me they enjoy our time after school together, but they have also learned so much during these activities. The modeling during our faculty meetings has our staff bringing similar learning experiences to their students. Experiences they gain knowledge from and will remember forever.

I've been the principal at my current school for the past 5 years. I've put a lot of hard work into creating and establishing the positive culture of a building I've always longed to work at. After five years I've come to the realization that working on improving culture is not a task I can check off of my To Do list and move on to the next. Culture is ongoing, it's always a work in progress. If we aren't continually working to keep it positive and moving forward, it can quickly revert.

As a leader, it's up to you to guide and shape the culture of your school. I encourage you to reflect on why you first got into education and then administration. Was it to sit, buried underneath paperwork and a computer screen for hours or to change the lives of students? We hold the power in what type of culture we establish in our buildings.

Jay has found a variety of ways to build staff relationships. Some of his favorites are individual conversations he has with staff to start out the school year. He asks each staff member the same three questions- What would you like Jay to keep doing? What would you like Jay to stop doing? What would you like Jay to start doing? The conversations last about 15 minutes and often divert from the three questions to the staff member's family or hobbies or challenges or celebrations.

Jay added a "halftime" discussion recently with each of his teaching staff. The teachers signed up for a 15 minute time slot and Jay asked them these three questions- What are you most proud of personally or professionally so far this school year? What can you celebrate about the school year so far? How can Jay support you for the rest of the school year? These conversations allowed the teachers to reflect and Jay got to share in the proud and celebratory moments. Some staff told Jay they just wanted more handwritten notes or

Voxer messages for support. Others wanted assistance with a struggling student or time to collaborate with a colleague. The bonus was that Jay got to spend 15 minutes alone with each teacher and provide a personal message about the great things that each of the teachers is doing in the school for students and their colleagues.

Challenge

Think about planning, or co-planning, a gathering that includes all staff members that allows for connecting and building positive relationships. Depending on the time of the year, this could be a back-to-school event, end-of-the-year celebration, or holiday inspired social event.

Chapter 21

Teachers (and Other Staff Members) Are Leaders, Too

(Ryan Sheehy)

When some think of leaders in schools their minds drift to thinking about superintendents, district level staff, or building level staff. However, there are so many leaders in a school that aren't front and center but offer the same level of leadership. We have all worked in schools where some of the most influential leaders didn't hold those titles at all. Anyone in a school, child or adult, can be a leader. All they need is support and a chance.

When I was a teacher I felt that teachers were always looked at like they aren't a leader and decided that it needed to change. Whenever I would go through a rough patch as a teacher, I looked for a way to lead and that would get me out of a funk and allow me to get back on task and lead in action. I would sit and write articles for different publications that would be printed throughout the world and it would allow me the opportunity to lead. As I wrote these articles some looked at me as a teacher in action, but not everyone. This was at a time that common core was the hot topic and teachers that did not know a lot about common core couldn't lead. So instead of giving more people excuses to tell me that I was not a leader, I enrolled myself in an online course from Stanford University all about common core. I wanted to be viewed as a leader.

Looking back on that time, I did not need to do those things in order to be viewed or even to be a leader. I was a leader because I was constantly looking for growth. I was a leader because I helped others become better. I was a leader because I was doing what was right for kids, not necessarily what was easy. I was a leader because I was a teacher in action.

Schools need to support teacher leaders. Our teachers have a passion for student learning and their own learning, and we need to provide teachers and other staff the opportunity to be leaders. Some teacher leaders have a focus on curriculum, some have a focus on the procedures within a school, and some have a focus on behavior. These teachers just need a chance to take on a leadership role so that they can share their ideas with others.

Jay had a group of teachers that wanted to take on student behaviors in their school. PBIS (Positive Behavior Interventions and Support) was the new buzz and this group of teachers wanted to give this new idea a try. Jay met with them and let them take the lead. They developed charts and expectations and consequences and rubrics and videos. They met with Jay again to show what they had put together. The teacher leaders were excited and ready to share with the entire staff. And then it happened. The teachers wanted Jay to lead the discussion. After a brief conversation, the teachers agreed to lead the conversation instead. Jay's reason- the teachers developed the ideas and they needed to share them with the staff. Jay would support them but he wasn't going to take the lead. Jay honestly felt that this teacher idea would be better accepted if the teachers shared it instead of if he shared it. Jay was there to support and encourage, but he wasn't there to lead. PBIS is still going strong in their school. Through reflection and discussion, changes have been made, but the changes have made the program even better for the students and the staff.

Mark noticed that there are teacher leaders who have talents, passions, and commitments for certain initiatives or projects. Mark is also blessed to have non-licensed staff members, clerical, paraprofessional, food service, who are leaders as well. Principals need to understand that everyone's voice needs to be heard and that everyone can be a leader. Mark's staff leaders have introduced and championed mobile maker carts and a transformation of the computer lab into an Innovation Lab. Teacher leaders continue to transform school culture and climate by leading PBIS initiations, our Equity Team, health and wellness efforts, the social committee, and other teams and committees that contribute to support for students, families, and colleagues.

Creating teacher leaders in your building not only helps the leader out, it shapes the culture of the school. It shows others that the leader is willing to have a shared leadership and willing to make sure everyone feels that they are working in a place where they are encouraged to grow.

Challenge

What ways do you encourage teacher and staff leaders? Are there things that you are currently doing as a principal that could be done better by a staff leader? How do you provide opportunities for your staff to be in action for their school and their students?

Chapter 22

Sharing and Telling Your School's Story

(Ryan Sheehy)

Being a leader on your campus allows you to share your school story from a perspective that you want to be told. Too often when people talk about a school or share a story about education it comes from a negative point of view. When you tell the story, the narrative is told the way you want it told from. You dictate the story that is being told about your school, district, and community.

On my first day as principal of an elementary school, I walked out onto the playground for 1st/2nd grade recess. To my surprise when I got to the field there was a man throwing a ball for his dog, right in the middle of the field with tons of kids playing. The school is connected to a community park and many community members felt that they could use the field whenever they wanted. I looked to one of the teachers and they indicated that this was a normal occurrence. Being my first day, I thought I would observe and take notes. Later that day I went out for another recess and it was a similar sight. This time there was a woman throwing a ball for her dog, right in the middle of kids playing a game of kickball. I had to do something, because it felt unsafe and I didn't like the thought of leaving kids vulnerable to whatever came through that park.

I contacted some central office leadership and put together a plan to make the campus more secure. To my surprise, less than one month later there was a fence put up between a neighborhood and the school, as well as the park and the school. Within hours of the new fence going up, we were receiving phone calls from neighborhood members upset about the fence. These people didn't have kids in the school and were upset about having to walk around the school to get to the park during school hours. No matter how much I talked to these people about the safety concerns that I was addressing they didn't want to listen, they didn't care. They wrote letters to my superintendent, the city mayor, and anyone who would listen. The community even held a neighborhood meeting with one thing on the agenda, me.

I knew that I needed to share my story in a different manner. Talking with community members and parents was not working. So I had students record a video on a green screen talking about the importance of the fence and keeping our students safe during the day. Once the video was recorded, we uploaded the video to a community forum on the next door app. This was where public perception completely changed. I allowed kids to share our story. We had control of the narrative and we were telling the story that people wanted to hear. We must share our story, otherwise, someone else will and it might not be the narrative that we want shared.

A school's story, frankly any story, is best told in pictures. Words can be misinterpreted. There are many ways to share pictures with our families and community. Social media apps like Instagram, Twitter, and Facebook are the apps that Jay uses to tell the school's story. Why three different apps? Jay finds that the students follow the school on Instagram, the educators he is connected with follow the school on Twitter, and the families and communities follow the school on Facebook. Each of these apps has its own purpose and Jay is able to share from all three using an app called If This Then That (IFTTT). Jay posts a photo and text on Instagram and, using applets on IFTTT, the photo and text are also posted to Twitter and Facebook. It's just that simple. There are even times when students ask Jay, "Can we be on mertonint (That's our Instagram account)?" Jay always replies with, "Show me some learning and I'll post it on Instagram!" The students always comply with that request.

Another way that Jay tells the school story is by using an online newsletter. Jay realized that the school newsletters rarely got home and important information and celebrations weren't being communicated in a timely manner. Once Jay started using the online platform, which is emailed home every Friday and posted on the school's Twitter and Facebook accounts, the families started getting information on time as well as seeing their children learning in school.

Share Your Story

Chris Legleiter, Middle School Principal, Overland Park, KS

Schools are rapidly changing across our country to best meet the needs of learners and prepare students for anything in their future. Educators should be commended for these efforts, as they are empowering learners, changing teaching practices and creating amazing experiences every day for students.

It is essential that leaders share and tell their school's story to help inform our society the positive impact of schools. Here are some ways to consider sharing this story.

Technology – This allows the school experience to be shared with others at any point in time and can reach all over the globe. Showing pictures and sending videos allow connections when Face-to-Face communication is not possible. Consider sharing: weekly newsletters via video instead of email; videos or pictures from classroom learning experiences; assemblies or special events so others can see the emotion, positivity and human connections that exist in schools; feedback measures from the community, as it is more timely and efficient.

Schools must partner with parents/guardians as we are developing their most precious commodity – their children. Leaders must be creative on keeping parents informed but more importantly have them experience this positive change in school by. Parent Panels leverage existing parents to share their child's school experience with parents that are new to your school. Student Showcases identifies specific nights where students demonstrate their learning from the classroom to their parents. This reinforces what teaching/learning looks like in our current age. Invite parents in to help lead activities that highlight parents' profession or serve as the audience to student presentations to make the learning authentic.

Create a Parent book study or EdCamp to help parents become familiar with resources, share conversations and learn together on raising children in this ever-changing world.

Involve the community to help our community understand how schools have changed. Many people still think of the school experience like it was when they went to school and that experience can be several generations ago. The school experience now has evolved considerably. Bring in professionals (ex. engineers, artists, doctors, farmers, and tradesmen) as ways to help explain a learning activity such as a PBL or Design Thinking. Their expertise is powerful for students making connections to the current world. Use an EdCamp model at "Back to School Night" or" Meet the Teacher" events to engage community partners to share their resources with families.

Students are the reason we have schools and they are cultivating the society we live in. Consider how can we have students share their experiences by: writing to other students (ex. pen pals) in different parts of the world; use Skype, blogs, or vlogs to connect with classes from different regions; or institute student-led conference in lieu of traditional parent-teacher conferences so students are empowered to own their learning.

Mark clearly remembers hearing George Couros say, "If you aren't telling your school's story, then somebody else will." That's true if you look at school reviews on websites such as GreatSchools.org, Niche.com and SchoolDigger.com and your school's rating from your state's Department of Education. You can control your school's narrative and how you present your school to your families, to the community, and to the world. When Mark got to his current school, he created a school Twitter hashtag to share the great things happening. He posts photos and encourages other staff members to do the same, to #GatewoodGators so others can see the great things happening.

Use your district's Communications Department and your community publications and invite reporters and photographers out to your school and evening events. That is something that's easy to do and something you can influence and control.

Challenge

Choose a platform to tell your school story and share it with the families and school community. Make sure to communicate the use of the platform to as many people as you can. What kind of impact does sharing your school story have on your school?

Chapter 23

Taking the Bus

(Ryan Sheehy)

Not everyone has the opportunity to drive the bus, like our fellow Oklahoma Principal In Action, Kas Nelson. However, most of us have the opportunity to ride the bus. Buses are a great way to learn about our students and a place to build relationships with students, families, and even staff.

When I wrote a blog post about the importance of leaders riding the bus, one of our district bus drivers came up to me and said they had read it and I always have an open invitation to ride their bus. My district doesn't offer bus transportation for any students other than those students in special education. At this point in time, I had 13 total students who rode the bus.

I was having an extremely busy week that seemed to never end. It was a go, go, go type of week that seemed to be filled with fires that needed to be extinguished. My wife was constantly checking in with me because I was showing signs of major stress at home. There was an issue that needed my attending to out in front of the school and I quickly went out there to make sure it was addressed. As I was working on that situation, the bus pulled up. Here came the kids that were going to ride that bus today, the bus that I was supposed to ride. I went over to the bus and greeted the driver and the aide like I do most days. One of the kindergarten students saw me coming off the bus and asked me if I would ride the bus with him. With my heart melting, I decided right then that I would! I radioed into the office to let them know I would be off campus and off we went.

Every stop, I would get off and chat with families and let them know how much we cherish their child. Some of the parents along the route were parents that I never got to see unless we were in a meeting together. I rotated seats around the bus, trying to sit next to all of the students individually. Some of my nonverbal students simply reached for my hand and just held it. Over the course of one and a half hours, I made connections with students but I also built a strong relationship with the driver and the aid on the bus. When I got off the bus, they said that was the first time that anyone had ever ridden with them and it would be something that they would never forget.

I hopped off the bus and headed back to the office. When I walked back into the office, I was met by two of the front office staff that looked at me with a big smile. They went on to say: "You really rode the bus. We thought you were kidding. Ryan, you are the most hands-on leader that we have ever seen." This adventure brought thoughts from so many people but it brought more to me than I can ever put into words. I created a bond with these kids that normally I do not get the opportunity to have or might not have made the time for.

Mark has ridden the school buses at various times. The first was for one of the early Principal In Action challenges and students and families members were surprised to see him on the bus. Mark had a great time sitting with different students (yes, Mark was a bad role model at times, sometimes he switched seats while the bus was moving), talking with them, and learning more about them. Most recently, bus riding has been to observe and watch the behavior of the bus riders. Of course, to no one's surprise, the behavior of the students on the bus when the principal is riding is perfect. Riding the bus not only demonstrates that you are a Principal In Action, it also sends a message of support to the bus driver when the principal is needed to be present, observe, listen, and learn.

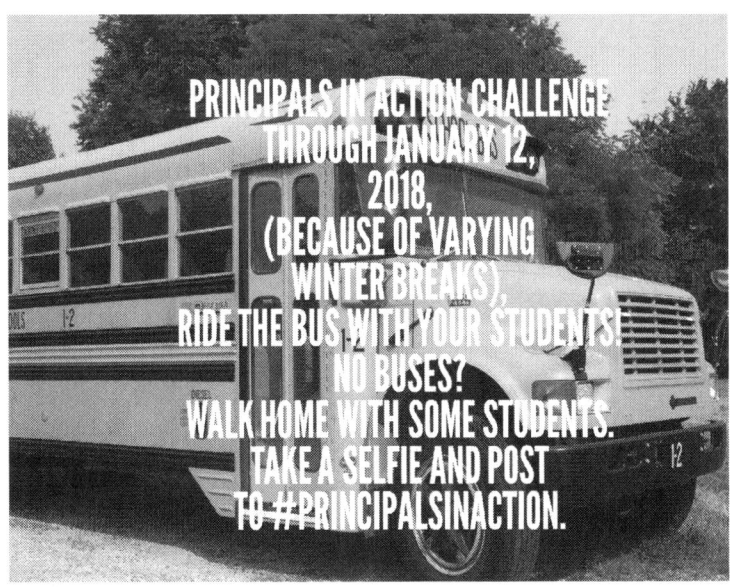

Jay has taken the opportunity to ride the buses from time to time. Most of the time it's because there has been an issue on the bus reported to him by the bus company or a student or family. But sometimes he'll just decide to hop on a bus just because it feels like a great day to connect with kids. Like Mark, Jay doesn't always follow the "stay in your seat while the bus is moving" rule, but it's important to not just sit in one seat or to not just sit next to the student that may have caused an issue to watch their behavior. Students like that you are seeing their house or apartment and the neighborhood they live in. You might actually get to better know what your school community looks like

Tips for riding the bus:

1. Strike up a conversation with your bus drivers about their personal life. Try to find out as much as possible to learn who they are and what they like to do.
2. Don't just sit next to the "naughty kids".
3. When the route is over, have a conversation with the driver.
4. End the ride by thanking the driver for getting the students to and from school safely.

Challenge

Get out and ride the bus with students. If your school doesn't use buses, create a walking school bus. Build connections with not only your students and community, but also the bus drivers and other staff.

Chapter 24

Reading to Classes and Students

(Ryan Sheehy)

Seeing a challenge amongst principals across the world to get into classrooms and read to students scared me as a high school administrator, until I did it. I saw friends and colleagues reading to classes all the time, but they were at the elementary school level, which I thought made more sense.

I decided that I would read to every English class. I looked for different books and came up with one that aligned with our goals as a school and something that we wanted to do. As I entered into the first classroom, kids looked at me like I was crazy, but as I began reading their faces changed. They were excited and became interested. They loved it! After the book was over the conversation heated up and we were able to have great dialogue about the meanings of the book and why we as a school would want to read it. Students were able to offer their opinions into meaning and debate as a class.

Moving to an elementary school principal position, I took the read-alouds with me. I tried to read to every class every month. The nice thing about reading to an entire school is that you can get the same message into every classroom in your school. Some months where it seems like my calendar was a nightmare, I read at lunchtime in our cafeteria, just so that every student gets to hear the book and I am able to share the love of literacy that I have with all of them.

Reading to classrooms wasn't enough. I wanted to include parents and families in the conversation. I needed to do more to share books with every child and their family. I decided that once a month, I would send home a read aloud video of me reading a book somewhere out in the community or in obscure places. The video would then be sent home via a digital newsletter. Parents and families would watch the video with their kids and it allowed for conversation about books and what the meanings were in the pages.

Mark has been inspired by great principal literacy leaders like Brad Gustafson, Liz Garden and Julie Bloss. For years, he has selected a book to read for the month, created a Google Spreadsheet for teachers to sign up for a 15 minute story reading time, and has read to as many classes that sign up. This is a great time to be a principal in action, connect with students, be in classrooms, and share your love of literacy. Thanks to ideas from others, Mark posts a picture of the current book he is reading to classes on his office door. When Mark first started this, he thought he had to select a book for primary students and another for intermediate classes. One month, when he started this practice, he was running short of time and grabbed the primary book to read to his 6th grade classes. They loved it! In fact, Mark has discovered that the upper elementary students are some of the best listeners and audiences. Mark's school-wide theme is "KIND - Keep It Nice Daily," and thanks to recommendations from other principals, Mark has discovered and has read stories that he connects to this theme. "Lady Pancake & Sir French Toast" is about trying not to compete, but work cooperatively. The books "Zero", "One" and "Two" by Kathryn Otoshi are about finding your place and feeling included. "Super Manny Stands Up," delivers a message about bullying, bystanders and friendships. If you are not reading to your students and sharing a love of literacy, this is an easy thing to accomplish in your journey to be a Principal In Action.

Read alouds are important for everyone. Jay enjoys being a part of the read aloud time in Language Arts classrooms, and sometimes other teachers do read alouds, too. Jay has been invited in to do a read aloud to classes during the Global Read Aloud. It's so great when he sees students who are excited about the book he is reading and are hanging on his every word. And this happens all the way up to the 8th graders. Jay has also recorded read alouds to share with the students during homeroom right after the announcements. These read alouds are sometimes the focus of an upcoming assembly or an all-school field trip. Jay recorded "We're All Wonders", the picture book that is based on the book "Wonder", the year that the movie of the same name came out. This was shared with the students in homerooms by all teachers. We later took the entire school to see the movie at a local theater. It was a great way to send the same message to all of the students and staff in the school. And yes, Jay did cry at the end of the movie.

There is another way to do read alouds - you can share a book using a live social media platform. Many Principals In Action members have done this for their schools either as a welcome back to school or on a school closing day. This option is another way to make connections with students and families as you can also discuss why you chose the book to share with your school community.

Challenge

Can you schedule time into the month to read to your students? If you need book ideas or suggestions, connect with @PrincipalFrench on Twitter and he will share his list of favorites with you.

Chapter 25

Balance Between Home and School

(Jay Posick)

Ryan, Mark, and I are in different places in our lives. Ryan is raising four children with his wife, Barbara, in California. Mark lives with his husband, Kip, in Minnesota. I live with my wife, Jenifer, and we are "empty nesters" in Wisconsin. We live three different lives, but we share the difficulties of having a balance between home and school. I would even tell you that the way the title of the chapter- balance between home and school- is written is an important way to get your focus in the right place. When Mark and I had our writing weekend (we spent a weekend in LaCrosse, the halfway point between where Mark and I live), we discussed the importance of this balance, realizing that it's important to work on this every day because every day has its balance challenges.

One thing I tell our staff is that family comes first. Sometimes I don't take my own advice and family comes second, or third. It's important to find ways to balance home and school and that includes a variety of ideas to make sure family is first. I have educator friends who take their school email off of their phone when they get home. I can't go to that level, but I do put a deadline on when I check school emails- 9:00PM. I jokingly say that nothing good happens on school email after 9:00, but I think it's true. I turn off all notifications at 9:00 and that allows me to spend at least one hour watching television or a movie with my wife. Checking an email after 9:00 that has a message from an upset staff member or family or student just doesn't work for me. It makes me restless and I don't sleep well. Ask my wife. If I don't sleep well I'm just not a nice person.

The phone is only one part of maintaining the balance between home and school. It's important to make sure that you have a date night with your spouse, significant other, or friends so that you can be someone other than the principal, even if only for a few hours. It's important to decompress and remove yourself from the life of being a principal once in a while. Have you ever been out grocery shopping and seen or heard people talking about you? Sometimes I think that people only see us as the principal and not as a person who needs to shop, and eat, and ride a bike, and play golf or anything else that "regular" people do.

I do remember not so long ago that our daughter, Lauren, was really into dancing. She had dance classes and participated in dance competitions locally, regionally, and nationally. But my favorite part of her dancing was the father/daughter dance routines. We actually thought that there should be a division for father/daughter dance routines at each of the competitions, especially the national competition. How does this fit into the balance between home and school? Dance was the one thing I shared with my wife and daughter, and although being a former basketball coach and wanting my daughter to play basketball, it's tough to admit that I really enjoyed watching Lauren dance. Those who know me will tell you that I am a cryer, and I'm alright with that. It's one of the many great things I inherited from my father. When I watched Lauren dance, or when I danced with her, nothing else mattered. And most of the time at the end of the dance I was crying.

Mark uses certain strategies to achieve a better home life and school life balance. One of those strategies includes having a bedtime of 9:00 pm. That is achievable most nights, but there is the occasional work or social commitment that interrupts that. But generally, Mark can stick to that routine. Going to bed at this time gives him eight hours of sleep with a wake-up time of 5:00 am. The morning time is when Mark reads email messages from the prior evening, plans and organizes his day, and slowly acclimates and gets ready.

You need to find a routine that works best for you, but don't neglect your sleep, meals, and activity level. A happy, healthy, and balanced principal will make for a happy, healthy and balanced school. Also, don't neglect your interests and passions. You may need to scale back at some point during the year, but don't eliminate the things that bring you joy and pleasure. One of Mark's passions is cooking. Now, the school week schedule and commitments are not always conducive to cooking during the week but Mark engages in his passion for cooking on the weekends and gets his fix for taking risks and being creative in the kitchen then.

Another strategy that you can use, and one that may be controversial, is having the ability to say, "No." I don't think you need to cancel a family commitment that was made a while ago when a work commitment comes up. I think it is okay to tell your music teacher that you are unable to attend the choir concert because it is the same night as your daughter's induction into the National Honor Society. Now, if it's important for you to deliver a welcome or message for an event you can't attend, can you create a short video welcoming everyone and apologizing for not being able to be there in person? Another strategy Mark uses is to communicate with staff that if it's something they really want him to attend, see, or be part of, let's work with Mark's schedule to make that happen. It's okay to use "No" to achieve more balance between your home and school lives.

Challenge

Revive your passions, interests, and hobbies. Reflect on something that you enjoy doing but haven't done in a while. Make it a priority and get back to enjoying something that you love.

Chapter 26

Getting Out of Your Office

(Jay Posick)

The mantra of #principalsinaction is "Get Out Of Your Office". It's on our wristbands as a reminder. Most of our challenges are centered around principals getting out of their offices. But looking at a wristband or taking on a challenge doesn't always create the daily habit of being out of your office. The daily habit of getting out of your office is created by getting out of your office. Sounds easy, doesn't it? But sometimes other things get in the way. The unexpected visit from a student, staff member, or family member of a student happens. There's a red light on your phone that means someone left you a voicemail. There are the five, ten or twenty emails that appear in your inbox that weren't there only a minute ago. There's the visit from the district office that then requires you to provide a report for a meeting you didn't know you were going to have that afternoon. You might need to fill in for a teacher who suddenly became ill and there is no one else to cover their class (this one really counts as getting out of your office but still limits the places that you can visit.).

I have found that scheduling time out of my office on my calendar means that I'll be out of my office. As the saying goes, if it's on your calendar it's going to happen. Have your assistant or secretary help you with this, if necessary. Your assistant or secretary can help you keep these "appointments" a priority. If you make getting out of your office such a priority that it's on your calendar, it becomes the first step in forming the get out of your office habit.

As you begin making this habit a priority, there may be some who are questioning why you are visiting classrooms or hanging out in the hallways or avoiding your office. They may ask you how you're getting all of your "principal work" done if you're not in your office. I would argue that the real "principal work" is getting into classrooms to see what learning is really going on. If you visit classrooms, the teachers and the students begin to expect it. I have made it such a habit that I visit an average of 20 classrooms a day out of the 27 classrooms in our school. If I don't visit a classroom, the teachers, and sometimes the students, ask me where I was. I'm invited into classrooms to see activities, to listen to presentations, to do read-alouds, and even to join in review games. One of our teachers uses the Circle of Power and Respect in his classroom and he often invites me to be a part of this amazing relationship building activity. If I'm not in classrooms and I'm not interacting with students and staff on a daily basis, I believe I don't really know what's happening in our school. And if I'm not interacting with students and getting to know them, there's no way I'd be invited into a Science classroom to do the Circle of Power and Respect (CPR). To do CPR right, you need to know your classmates (if you're a student) and students (if you're an educator).

So you may be asking, "Jay, how can you be out of your office for most of the day?" The answer for me is a simple one and it's actually a question right back at you. "Why wait in your office for situations to come to you when you can get out of your office and meet the situations head on?" I start my day receiving an email that lists any staff members who are absent. That's where my visits begin, checking in on our guest teachers and letting them know that I'm a phone call away if they have any questions or have any issues. They know to call the office and my secretary will text me and I'm in their classroom within minutes. I also am in classrooms enough to know when one class might be a little more challenging for a guest teacher. Although it might not be completely apparent, the behavior of students and adults changes when the principal is in the room. Some of that is my title and some of that is the relationships I build, especially with some of our most challenging students. If those students only see me in my office, it's not really the most stable relationship. Just like we tell teachers that students won't care about your class unless you show them you care about them, the same is true for principals. If the only relationship you have with a student is disciplinary in nature, that's just not enough. Find out about their interests and hobbies and friends and family. Getting to know students and showing them you care is really the only way to get poor behavior to change, and that relationship building just can't happen only in the principal's office.

So here's a strategy I've used to help build those

relationships. It's called "2 x 10" and stands for 2 minutes 10 days in a row. Find that student or students that you know can be challenging or that you just haven't connected with yet. Spend 2 minutes (at least) with them for 10 days in a row. Let them lead the conversation. Find out what they want to talk about and just listen. If you know something about their topic, add some of your own thoughts. If you don't know anything about the topic just listen. As soon as the 2 minutes is up, move on and write or leave yourself a note about what you discussed. If you know nothing about the topic, spend a few minutes that night finding out something about their chosen topic. Showing an interest in what a student likes can start to build that relationship. It doesn't need to be just 2 minutes for 10 days, either. You can extend the amount of time and the number of days. Just don't have that conversation in your office. No principal really makes a connection with a student in their office. Make those connections in the hallway, in the cafeteria, or at recess. You'll be amazed at what you'll learn about the student just by letting him or her lead the conversation. The connection might not happen the first day or even the fifth day, but the consistent conversations over 10 days will really let the student know that you care about him or her.

You may be asking how people find me when I'm not in my office. I don't use a walkie talkie or carry a school issued phone when I leave my office. Our school secretary, who really knows where everyone is, can find me with a text message. Walkie talkies and school phones disturb the classrooms too much, unless I put in an earpiece like the Secret Service. My cell phone is on vibrate so a text or email or Google message or direct message on Twitter get my attention. Our superintendent knows to send me a Google message if he wants a response to a question or needs to meet with me about something. How about those voicemails from parents? They go right to my email, complete with caller ID so that I can listen to them on my cell phone in the hallway or return to my office if it's a phone call I have, or haven't been expecting.

Mark looks at the positives and benefits of being out of the office. He often talks about being able to observe systems and monitor and adjust as needed. Being on the playground allows Mark to interact with students, connect with playground supervisors, see what activities students are engaged in, and check out the conditions on the grounds of the building. Spending time in the cafeteria allows Mark to pay attention to the adult/student relationships, observe the flow of students entering and exiting, and watch student interactions and behavior. Being out of his office allows Mark to see how he can support, enhance, and improve school systems.

Some of you might be asking yourself: "What if people complain about the leader not being in their office?" Ryan has been in many meetings where it has been brought up that the building principal should be in the office. Ryan is quick to respond and share that the entire building is his office. There is no reason that leaders need to be sitting in their offices. We all have computers in our pockets and are accessible at the drop of a hat. The smartphone has changed accessibility to leaders and has changed the way that they can lead. No leader needs to be sitting in their office.

A friend told me a story recently about working in the central office. He said he would go into the office everyday and would hear the conversations that were happening about kids and about school. The friend made it a point to be out of their office and out at the school sites with the students and staff that need support. This person would go back and different office staff would comment that they had not seen him in quite some time. His response would always be the same, " That's a good thing. That means I am doing my job."

You would often be in meetings at the central office when the conversation would go to a place of talking about what was happening in the classrooms. What the instruction looked like and how the kids were interacting with the text and formulating responses. The problem with these conversations is that without visiting the sites and getting out of their offices, they truly had a misunderstanding of what was happening. What they thought the trends were, what they thought was happening in the classroom was actually not happening. They had lost touch with reality. As a leader, in the school/at the district level/ or anywhere for that fact we must stay in touch with those we lead. If we spend our time trying to fix things that don't need to be fixed or problem solving problems that are not there, we are just wasting our time. We can do better!

Challenge

Try the 2x10 strategy with a student, spending 2 minutes with a student for 10 days in a row. Let the student lead the conversation. Show a real interest in them and what they are sharing with you. And once you have connected with that student, try it again with another student. Spending the time getting to know the student, with no strings attached, will certainly make their day.

Chapter 27

Admit Your Vulnerabilities

(Mark French)

You may wonder why there is a chapter on admitting your vulnerabilities in a book on redefining the role of a principal and being proactive in getting out of your office. For me, it took a long time to admit my vulnerabilities. I wanted to be perfect, make no mistake, and do everything right. Well, that is not possible and is an unattainable dream. Just like we do for our students and staff members, we want to help them discover their strengths and areas for growth, make a place to support their growth, and provide feedback for reflection and processing, principals need to do the same thing. Through feedback from others, self-reflection, and working with a professional coach, I was able to work through things that were blind spots for me. One of those was, although I felt I was a principal in action for my students (greeting them in the morning, joining them on the playground, reading to classrooms), I was missing being a principal in action for my staff members. I needed to admit my vulnerability in that I was focusing on students and missing making connections with staff members.

You must be willing to admit your vulnerabilities so you can take action on growing and improving. Being a Principal In Action is about supporting all of the segments of your school: students, families, community members, and staff members. One way I admitted, and modeled, my vulnerabilities, was to share with my staff. One year, after a particularly difficult round of anonymous survey feedback, after taking time to reflect, I shared my feelings with my staff. I told them that it was difficult to read many of the comments, that I had to dig deep and reflect on my part and take responsibility, and that I had to address my weaknesses in order to change and grow.

It is not easy to stand in front of others and admit your vulnerabilities and to be open and honest, but it is these kinds of actions from principals that will help develop trust and strengthen relationships. Other actions I have taken include sharing my story "Why I Am a Champion of the Underdog" from a MESPA Speaks Talk I gave to my elementary principal colleagues and presenting my racial autobiography that I shared with my district colleagues during our Courageous Conversations learning. I had to realize that if I am willing to be vulnerable and share with others, I need to model and do the same thing for my staff.

Being vulnerable isn't easy. It takes a great deal of courage to share those things that mean the most to you. Jay's staff would tell you that he can be emotional, sometimes crying in front of students or staff during assemblies or meetings. Jay shares personal stories as well as stories about family and friends. He also finds videos that he knows will have an impact on students or staff, sometimes leading to tears. A number of staff members ask Jay to give a disclaimer when sharing these videos. One example of Jay sharing a personal message was at a Veterans Day ceremony, run completely by the National Junior Honor Society, in front of the entire student body, staff, Veterans, and their guests. Students and staff are chosen to share a letter that they had written to a member of their family who served our country in the military. For the first ever Veterans Day ceremony, Jay was selected. He wrote a letter to his father who served in the Navy during the Korean War. As is almost always the case, Jay became emotional sharing the letter, crying during nearly the entire reading. He showed his real emotions, in front of everyone, and he didn't apologize. After the assembly was over, one of the guests came up to him and said, "Don't ever apologize for crying about your family. It's great for the kids to see that, even though you are older, it's alright to show the love you have for your family."

Don't hesitate to let your students and staff see that you are a real person with emotions and feelings. Model that vulnerability and it will help you develop even stronger relationships with your students and staff.

Ryan thinks back to when he was earning his teaching credential and the professors often reminded the class about not sharing any personal stories or connections with students. He held on to that advice for some time. The longer that he taught the more he realized that it was bad advice. As educators/leaders, we must use our own personal vulnerabilities and share those with our students and with those that we lead to humanize ourselves and help others grow. Ryan often tells stories from when he was an NCAA cross country runner in college. He was not a strong runner, but really wanted to be part of a team and the school needed more guys. The vulnerability that Ryan shows when sharing these stories with staff and students allows him to connect and show others that you don't always have to be great at something, but you do need to try.

Challenge

Being vulnerable isn't easy, but it sends a powerful message to those you serve. Share a personal story with a student or staff member that will help them get to know you better than they know you now. Obviously, you determine how personal the story is and then reflect on how sharing that story impacted your relationship with the people with whom you shared it.

Chapter 28

Ask for Help

(Mark French)

Principals In Action can't do it all, and even they need to ask for help at times. Fortunately for me, through lots of learning, I've figured out ways and resources to ask for the help I need. As mentioned earlier, principals, and educators in general are fearful of being vulnerable, admitting their weaknesses, and asking for help. In discussions with staff members who I work with through the formative and summative observation process, I tell them that I actually see asking for help as a strength and not a weakness. What it indicates to me is that someone has reflected, recognizes something is off, have run out of ideas, so now they need to seek advice, support, or help. Acknowledging that, being a reflective practitioner, and using your tools, resources, and networks is a virtuosity. I've figured out ways and resources to ask for help.

Admitting I need help is the first step. Then I look to my support systems to talk about and ask for that help. Is it something happening at home or with our family schedule and commitments that I need to talk to my husband about? Have we overcommitted and need to alter our plans? Kip, my husband, has certainly come through for me whether it's cooking and delivering the taco meat to school for the conference meal I'm providing for the staff or shopping for the Oreo cookies I need the next day to celebrate National Oreo Cookie Day with my staff.

When I need help I also lean on our administrative assistant. She uses her virtuosities to help me with projects, ideas, events, and activities. She is a hard worker who jumps in whether it's setting up tables for our monthly Citizens of the Month celebration or organizing the set-up for a school literacy night.

It's important to know the skills and talents of your family members, work colleagues, and members of your PLN, so you can reach out to the best person for some specific needs. One of my sisters is a great organizer and planner and she is the one I reach out to help plan family get togethers, vacations, and celebrations. I think I am a great idea person, but I need those around me to help execute my ideas, who are agreeable and willing to help, and who I can rely on.

Building my PLN has given me a whole new group of colleagues and friends to reach out to and ask for help. Most often I lean on the members of the Principals In Action (PIA) Voxer group. Voxer is a great tool to connect with others to share your successes and challenges. The members of the PIA Voxer group reach out to each other to ask for advice and ideas to spice up kindergarten orientation, address schoolwide culture and climate, or support a particularly challenging student. I am always asking my PLN for help because they have been there, have experienced the same things, and can listen and share their perspectives.

Jay has had to ask for help more times than he can admit. He has asked for help regarding students, staff, and school culture. There are so many things that a principal needs help with that others have already gone through. Why not use those people you know to provide guidance and suggestions with a challenge? Mark mentioned the PIA Voxer group as one of his "go-to" groups of colleagues, and Jay wouldn't disagree. Because Jay is a middle school principal, Jay reaches out to his middle school principal Voxer group often. They discuss student issues, staff issues, and school issues. They know each other well enough that they also discuss family issues. This Voxer group has principals from Alaska to Connecticut and many states in between. Although Jay hasn't met every member of this group, he knows that he can rely on them for just about anything.

But sometimes you need to ask for help from those with whom you work. That can be difficult because you are being vulnerable by admitting that you just don't have the answer to the issue. Jay has a group of teachers that make up the Building Leadership Team. They meet once a month with an open agenda. They start with shout outs, move on to concerns, and end up with topics to discuss. It's in these meetings that Jay asks for help with those things that will have an impact on the school and, more specifically, the school's culture. Building relationships with these teacher leaders has allowed Jay to ask questions that, when solved, will have a more positive outcome for the school. We cannot "do school" alone. It's so important to ask for help.

Keep Looking For the Answers

Kim Griesbach, Principal, Shiocton, WI

I have had the privilege to be in education for 29 years working with so many wonderful elementary and middle school children and amazing educators and leaders! When I look back on my journey, I have so many people who have helped me grow, inspired me, challenged me, pushed me out of my comfort zone, provided me with new ideas, and helped me strive to be my "best self" on a daily basis. These people I consider to be part of my PLN (Personal Learning Network).

Being the only elementary/middle school principal in my district, I needed to find ways to connect with others around my area, region, and state. That is why attending conferences became so important to me. Conferences and other professional development opportunities have always been a part of my journey as a leader. The connections I have made and the information I have obtained along the way has been second to none. However, I can honestly say that I have never felt more connected as I do right now at this point in my career through my involvement with Twitter.

Never did I think that Twitter would become my best source of networking, sharing of ideas, inspiration, and professional development and would provide me with an incredible support system during this phase of my career. I owe my first steps to Eric Sheninger who I heard speak at a state convention in 2013. Eric encouraged every person in the room to create a Twitter account. Because of this, I am now connected to people involved in education all around the world. I am connected to people I have heard speak at conventions and authors of educational books that I have read. I have been inspired to read other educational books due to seeing information and book discussions on Twitter.

Twitter is how I was introduced to the book Be the One by Ryan Sheehy and Kids Deserve It by Todd Nesloney and Adam Welcome. Within their books, these authors encourage the reader to Tweet out reflections to various questions. I began small by observing, but eventually began Tweeting my reflections and participating in Twitter chats.

Twitter connected me to Jay Posick who I now connect with during Twitter chats. While attending the same convention, Jay (spontaneously) asked me to join in and present with him during a particular session. This is what I absolutely love about my PLN - - people like Jay are pushing me out of my comfort zone, challenging me to get out of my office, challenging me to try new things, inspiring me to keep playing my morning music in the hallways, connecting me to other vibrant leaders, and are helping me grow immensely! Via Twitter, I am connected to a wonderful, diverse group of people in education every single day.

As I said earlier, I have been in education for a very long time, yet, I feel I am more connected than ever and am learning and growing more than ever before. I encourage every one of you to connect with others - - in whatever way you feel comfortable, but don't be afraid to try something new. There no longer should be anyone in education sitting in their classroom or office and working in isolation. My wish for every principal and person in education is to establish a connection, lifelong learning, support, inspiration, reflection, growth, and most of all...tremendous joy.

Ryan loves being a principal in this era. There is no need to be alone. Being in a connected time in the world has shown Ryan that he can literally reach out and ask questions at anytime and receive answers from all over the world. He especially enjoys hearing responses from other places in the country and how they would handle a situation. This allows for great dialogue and collaboration amongst leaders. Asking for help allows others to realize that it is okay not to know everything and it is okay.

When Ryan interviewed for the position of principal he talked about his background when it comes to instruction. Ryan prided himself on being someone that can build a strong school culture, but not necessarily big on curriculum. One of the areas was highlighted was the fact that Ryan admitted his area of weakness and knew how to ask for help.

There is so much to learn in education and so little time. You do not need to know everything, however, you do need to know how to ask questions.

Challenge

Think about three people you can ask for help: a family member, a work colleague, and a friend from your professional network. Find a way to thank these folks for what they do for you and mean to you.

Chapter 29

Get Others Involved

(Mark French)

When I think back, I was encouraged to attend conferences and become active in my state principals' association by one of my former principals who was a mentor and friend. A principal colleague in another district has been a role model and mentor in helping me use technology for learning and engagement. Another friend got me connected with the Voxer group Principals In Action which has led to reflection, learning, ideas, support, and friendships.

Most of my life and career, it has taken someone noticing something in me or wanting to share an opportunity with me to inspire and motivate me. I try to do this with others. I learned from a great Superintendent the idea of "spearfishing." She used this term to describe the act of identifying a particular individual you need or want to recruit for a task and going and directly asking them. I use this strategy when I need to involve and engage others. Sometimes the general ask, inviting everyone to step up, volunteer, and get involved, doesn't work. I think the general ask doesn't always work because people are reluctant and are looking for a specific invitation or request. I have found it powerful to "spearfish" and make a personal overture when looking to get others involved.

One of my district elementary principal colleagues is in his third year as principal and he is dynamic, personable, and full of energy. Our state association was looking for someone to serve as president-elect for our western suburban division. I don't think my colleague would have responded to a general ask, for a variety of reasons, but I recognized his leadership qualities and personal characteristics that would make him a great division president-elect. I spearfished and asked him if he would be interested and willing to take on this responsibility and he said, "Yes." Now we have a great leader helping to guide the work of our division.

Jay has been a member of AWSA, the Association of Wisconsin School Administrators, for over 15 years. He has presented with colleagues at a number of their conferences and has always enjoyed the connections that he has made. Recently, Jay was asked to share the Principals In Action message at SLATE (School Leaders Advancing Technology Education) after a speaker had a conflict and was unable to attend. Jay didn't want to be the only person sharing this message so he reached out to Kim Griesbach, a principal from Shiocton, Wisconsin, to ask her to help share the message. She reluctantly agreed, but showed up to the session ready to help out in any way. With Jay's jammypack playing music, Kim greeted the attendees at the door. The session was well attended, even though the description hadn't made it into the program. And by the way, Jay and Kim had never met in person before they attended the SLATE conference. Reaching out and specifically asking someone is such a powerful way to get others involved.

Ryan has presented at the district/county/state level as a teacher and as an administrator. As a teacher leader, Ryan always found it important to his own growth as an educator and as a way to motivate him each and every day to become a better person and educator. While presenting at the state level, Ryan would look to other teachers to motivate them to come with him and watch at first. Once he gave them the opportunity to watch the first year, they would gain the comfortability to present the following year.

Fast forward 10 years and Ryan talks with leaders all over the world and encourages them to get involved. Getting involved not only allows you to share your knowledge with others, but it is the relationships that are built through the sharing process that gives you resources that will help you throughout your career.

Challenge

Think about and "spearfish" a colleague to join your state's association, attend an EdCamp with you, or sign up for a professional development activity together. Find colleagues and friends that you can personally get involved.

Chapter 30

Work to Replace Yourself

(Mark French)

I know principals who are reluctant to be out of their schools connecting with others, attending conferences, and engaging in professional development. Since I started my administrative career, I've found it necessary and important to continue learning and growing. I never want to be stagnant. Even as a teacher, I purposefully threw away bulletin board designs because I didn't want to recycle the same ideas year after year. I figured my students were new each year and deserved current, applicable bulletin boards, lesson plans, activities, and experiences. I've carried that belief into my principalship. I need to stay current, purposeful, and meaningful. The title of this chapter, "Work to Replace Yourself", means that you need to create a team, empower others, and develop systems so things operate smoothly when you are not there.

If I need to be out of my building for district and state commitments or my own professional development, I need to ensure decisions are made, systems operate, and learning continues in my absence. One way I do this is by meeting with key team members, having discussions, making decisions, and communicating those decisions. I have worked with members of our office team to determine who makes which types of decisions in my absence. We've decided, and have communicated, that the administrative assistant makes operational decisions, the student support specialist makes student management decisions, and the counselor makes staff and parent decisions, in consultation with my neighboring back-up principal as necessary. Sometimes I think, "don't others already know this?" I've found that the answer is, "no." I've learned that I need to share my principal thinking and actions more broadly with others so they have accurate information.

Jay meets weekly with grade level and specials teams to discuss a variety of topics, including when he will be out of the building or out of the district. Jay works in a small Kindergarten through eighth grade district of about 850 students. His superintendent is almost always available to help out in his absence, but the teachers in the school know the procedures that are in place for behavior as well as building procedures in case the superintendent isn't available. There isn't only one teacher who knows about these procedures. All of the teachers know the procedures and are able to step in to take over in my absence. Our instructional assistants and custodians also know the building procedures and help out when needed. When Jay is gone for an administrative team meeting or out at a conference, he feels completely confident that the school will run smoothly.

Jay also relies heavily upon his secretary when he is away from school. She knows that Jay will check in at least once a day so she can give him an update, but she also sends a text message or email if something needs to be addressed right away. To be completely honest, Jay's secretary rarely reaches out to him when he is out of school because the teachers and other staff can take care of nearly everything without him. Is Jay concerned about that? Not at all. It makes him feel that the school belongs to the students and staff and not to Jay. Isn't that what we'd all like to feel?

Ryan works hard to ensure that the school runs smoothly with or without him on campus. The goal of any leader should be to build capacity and trust, so that when the leader leaves for the day or permanently things run effectively and efficiently. There should not be things that rely only on the leader to get done. Once you create your team and build capacity in all members, everyone can work together and accomplish any of the tasks. One of Ryan's goals as a leader is to not be needed.

Principals need to be out of their buildings for professional development, district commitments, sick days, family illness, personal leave, etc. We must develop others, create systems, and communicate so decisions are made and things continue to operate smoothly in our absence. Being proactive and planning ahead will make it much easier and will help your staff know what to do.

Challenge

Have a conversation with a member of your staff that you know has the ability to take over for you in your absence. Let them know that you have faith in them. Then sign up for a conference and leave this staff member in charge, and don't contact with them while you're gone until the school day is over. How did it go?

Chapter 31

Dust Off Your Teaching Skills

(Jay Posick)

Recently, it's been difficult to find enough guest teachers to fill in for sick staff or instructional assistants. Sometimes those responsibilities fall on teachers during their preparation periods, but that doesn't always fill all of the spots. More and more I have been called on to cover for a class period or two, but I have also needed to fill in for the entire day. In those times, it's vital to make sure that you keep up with the teaching skills and techniques that are being utilized by our teachers. It has been 17 years since I was a classroom teacher, but by being in classrooms every day and joining in on professional development opportunities, I can dust off and improve upon my teaching skills so that the students still get the benefit of a good learning environment.

With touch screen interactive boards, Chromebooks, and other devices, if I was to be living in the world of 1987 technology, the first year I taught, I'd be slighting our students.

Even if I used my teaching ideas from 2002, my last year of teaching, the students would be slighted. They deserve more than my ancient techniques. So much has changed in the classroom in the nearly 20 years since I last taught in my own classroom. No longer are there chalkboards or overhead projectors. We have more options for flexible seating and learning spaces. The students deserve the benefits of the internet, conversations with each other in class, and a variety of other things that frankly weren't techniques I utilized while I was teaching. While being in classrooms helps me see how our teachers are teaching and how our learners are learning, it is even more important for me to be involved in our teachers' professional development.

When we have professional development opportunities, I do my best to be an active part of the learning. I have been fortunate to attend professional development in New York City (Remember, I'm from Wisconsin) for our Language Arts curriculum with our classroom and special education teachers. It's vital to attend sessions with our teachers and to make the time to meet with them to discuss how I can support them in the classroom and provide them feedback after classroom visits. When we have professional development and training in our district, I'm joining the staff as much as I can so that I can learn the new curriculum and techniques that will benefit our students. It also gives me points of reference for conversations with our teachers after classroom visits and formal observations. It is so helpful to have those common points of reference for conversations, and it also helps me to put these techniques into action when I'm covering a class. Dust off your teaching skills and put them into action.

Mark gets the opportunity to dust off his teaching skills when there is a shortage of guest teachers, if staff members need to come in late or leave early because of other commitments, or if a teacher needs to be relieved to attend a meeting. Whenever Mark dusts off his teaching skills and teaches in a classroom, he is reminded of what a great job teachers do and how important it is to support them. Earlier in the school year, Mark covered in a third grade classroom during literacy time. His district had adopted a new literacy curriculum and Mark had been observing teachers implement that. But, this was his first opportunity to deliver instruction using the new curriculum. Thankfully, the third grade teacher was extremely organized and well planned, because Mark sure did have a tough time with the new curricular concepts. Working with the third graders gave Mark an appreciation for the teachers who were having to implement the new curriculum and he was able to advocate for more planning and professional development time for them.

It is important as a leader in any business, school, or life too show others that you are not too far removed from the skill in that company. In education, Ryan feels that the leaders should be in the classroom and should be willing to drop everything and teach. Schedules often get in the way, but Ryan loves the opportunity of getting in and co-teaching a lesson or simply modeling the lesson for others. When a leader gets into the "trenches" and is willing to be vulnerable others take notice and are generally more willing to do the same thing. Ryan has seen great power in allowing classroom teachers the time to observe him teach in a different way. Having a background being a physical education teacher, not all classroom teachers felt Ryan had the know-how of to instruct in a 4 wall classroom.

Taking the time to dust off his teaching practices and modeling different practices have changed that perception. Ryan also takes advantage of all professional development days as a time to model instructional strategies that he would like to see on a daily basis in the classroom.

Challenge

If you aren't one of the first volunteers to substitute in the classroom when you lack guest teachers, make that a priority. If that isn't a need for your building, find ways to cover for your teachers by volunteering to teach a lesson or even co-teach with them. You will see your classroom credibility increase.

Chapter 32

Make It Work For You

(Mark French)

I have been privileged to share the Principals In Action message and philosophy with others locally, across Minnesota, and at the national level. During a recent presentation at the Minnesota Elementary School Principals' Association Winter Institute with my friend and colleague, Principal J Kapuchuck from Virginia, we shared strategies for being a principal in action. As I watched some of the participants taking notes and writing down resources, I reflected back to professional development sessions and conversations with other leaders whom I admire, who inspire me, and who I want to be like. I remembered that you have to make being a principal in action work for you.

I used to feel inadequate because I wasn't blogging regularly, wasn't creating video announcements, or wasn't getting into classrooms on a regular basis to interact with students and provide feedback to teachers. Then, I had to stop comparing myself to others and remember I have virtuosities that others see in me.

When I think about making it work for you (or me), I think back to my Twitter journey and experience. When I joined Twitter, it was overwhelming to me and I saw others doing wonderful things and sharing their Tweets. How could I get to that level? How are they able to do that? I'm not worthy. I had to stop that thinking that way and focus on what I could do. After learning from George Couros at the TIES conference in Minneapolis in December of 2013, he challenged us to tell our school's story and to become comfortable with social media. After hearing George, I committed to finding one thing happening in my school each day, take a photo, and share that on Twitter. It became a challenge and scavenger hunt for me because I wanted to showcase all of our teachers and students, so I was on the lookout for great stories.

An online principal friend, Principal Greg Moffitt from California, recently Tweeted, "On the really tough days, when I start looking for the positive, I start seeing it everywhere." That is such a true and wise statement. When I set out on the mission of finding amazing, simple, engaging things to share happening in my school, I started seeing them everywhere. My point is that I started small and took one step at a time. It started with seeing positive things happening in my school, to sharing multiple Tweets a day, to starting the hashtag #GoodNewsCallOfTheDay, to participating in Twitter chats (just lurking at first), to leading Twitter chats, to learning from educators all around the country and world, to exploring and using other social media platforms like Voxer, Instagram, and Facebook to connect, learn, and share our story.

It would never be possible to do all the things that every principal does. Some things fit while others don't, and that's just fine. Jay likes to take ideas and "Mertonize" them (from his city in Merton, WI, thus the term "Mertonize".). He knows that he can't do everything; it's just not possible or practical. Some principals drive the school buses, but Jay isn't licensed to drive a bus so he can only ride the buses. Covering recess for the teachers isn't a possibility for Jay because the teachers don't have recess duty. Jay does do recess duty every day, though, as it is one responsibility he has taken from the teachers. Sometimes Jay hears an idea on the Voxer chat or reads an idea on the #principalsinaction Twitter hashtag and tries to find a way that he can do that in school.

Here's the deal. Pick one or two or three things and do them really well. It might be stopping in every classroom every day. It might be picking one day to spend in one grade level for the entire day. It might be spending an entire morning out of your office. There are those principals that can spend an entire day out of their office, but that just might not work for you, and that's okay. Find what works for you, "Mertonize" it like Jay does to fit your school environment, and then get better at those things every day.

School buildings across the world are very different. Ryan looks at his community, his students, and his staff to see what needs to be done at his school and his buildings. Do not start doing things, because that is what everyone else is doing. Look around and see what needs to be stronger in the classroom for kids, making sure that whatever you decide to change or do impacts learning. Culture impacts learning, but you also don't need to start doing everything you see on Twitter to impact the culture. Ryan believes that are big things that impact and there are smaller impactors. We all have such limited time, we really need to make sure that the time we do spend has a big impact.

Challenge

Pick one thing you've gleaned from the book or that you've seen or heard other principals do and weave that into your practice. Pick one thing, follow through, be consistent, and do it well. Then add on other practices as you are able.

Chapter 33

How Can I Help?

(Jay Posick)

One of the things that principals get to do is have conversations with those they serve. Sometimes the conversations are pretty easy and sometimes they can be difficult. Mark and I were having a discussion at lunch one day when we were spending a weekend writing. Mark and I were discussing conversations with staff when they come to you to provide you with information. Sometimes it's a chance for the staff to vent, sometimes they want you to solve the problem, and sometimes they want to solve the problem with you. The tricky part is finding out which of those options is the desired outcome. As Mark and I continued our conversation, we discovered that the option can be found by just asking, "How can I help?"

Our conversation really was around the question we normally ask in these situations, "What would you like me to do?" But think about that question. It can mean many things based upon how the person you are speaking with interprets it. Here are at least five ways that this can be heard, with the first being the way it is meant and each of the others having added emphasis on one word which may lead to hurt feelings or misunderstandings.

What would you like me to do?

What would you like me to do?

What would ***you*** like me to do?

What would you like ***me*** to do?

What would you like me to ***do***?

I shared with Mark that my wife, Jen, and I like watching *New Amsterdam*, a television show on the NBC network. Dr. Max Goodwin, the main character, has taken over as the medical director of a New York City hospital. He asks one question at least once every episode, "How can I help?" I shared that question with Mark and his expression was amazing. Those four words can't be taken in any way other than as a person who has listened and now wants to help.

I have used this question often after student, staff, and family conversations and have received a variety of answers from "I just needed to vent" to "I just wanted you to be aware" to "Thanks for listening" to "Can you help me come up with a solution?" to "I need your help". The moral of the story- It's not about me, it's about them, and if you ask, "What would you like me to do?" it becomes about me instead of about them. If you change the question to "How can I help?", it puts the focus on the other person. And sometimes we need to realize that we just need to listen and not say anything at all. My dad and many others have told me that I have two ears and one mouth for a reason. I need to remember that more often.

Mark learned a valuable lesson many years ago in how to ask the right question. One of his 4th grade teachers stood in his office door describing yet another frustrating interaction with one of her students. Mark listened intently, nodded to signal he was understanding, and let the teacher talk without interrupting her. After she was finished, Mark processed quickly and thought to himself, *She knows this student so well and she knows what she has already tried*. So, he asked (thinking he was offering his support), "What would you like me to do about it?"

Mark remembers the teacher looking at him then she turned and walked away. Mark was confused and called her back to clarify. While Mark thought he was offering his support and wanted to hear her suggestions, she heard him brush the situation off and not take any responsibility for helping. After a little while, Mark was able to clarify that he valued her input and opinion and wanted to take her suggestions. As Jay pointed out earlier, this question is easy to misunderstand. Mark has since tried to change his approach by asking, "How can I help?"

Challenge

After having a conversation with a student, staff member, or family, ask the question that's the title of this chapter, "How can I help?" Take note of the reaction of the other person and how it makes them feel. Try to use this question in as many conversations as you can, including those you might have with your family.

Chapter 34

When You Need to Be a Principal In Action in Your Office

(Mark French)

While it is important for a building leader to be out of the office learning, observing, listening, interacting and being visible, sometimes it is necessary to be a principal in action in the office. During a recent Principals In Action Voxer group chat and challenge, principals checked in, talked about, and shared photos of how they were redesigning and rethinking their office spaces.

When I arrived at my current school, the principal's office was a cluttered, dark, and shut off space. There were blinds pulled down covering the windows to the office area (which have since been removed), there was a huge section of the desk in which the principal sat on one side and anyone else sat on the other (that desk has been removed and was replaced by a round table), and a variety of shelves were covered by knick-knacks and other tchotchkes (I removed the shelves to create a more open space). I have since redesigned my office space to include two chairs and a bookcase (put together by four 6th grade helpers). The bookcase is filled with children's books, there is an open space on the floor to engage students in coding and programming robots, and a drawer in my desk is filled with puzzles, games, and activities for students to help calm and refocus them.

I would rather students sit on the orange covered chairs in my office than be lined up outside my office waiting for me. I have tried to create an attractive environment for the work that we principals conduct with students, families, and staff members.

Jay's office is not much bigger than a walk-in closet and has only one window, and that's a skinny one in the office door. One wall of the office is shared by the staff bathrooms (no added comment necessary) and the acoustical ceiling does little to keep the sound of his office from going into the nearby conference room or visa versa. The main office is a much larger and lighter space that is occupied by one secretary, a window out to the foyer, and windows out to the commons/cafeteria. The office space has become a place to store items and isn't very welcoming. There is discussion about an office redesign but that is down the road a year or more. With that being said, there are times, mostly in the morning before school and in the afternoon after school that Jay will spend time in the office. Observations need to be written, phone calls need to be made, emails need to be answered, and conversations need to be had. Being a principal in action can happen in an office, but the office needs to be a welcoming place, even if the conversations that happen are difficult or uncomfortable.

Not much can be done at this time to change Jay's office, but when changes will be made, Jay is sure to have a say in how the office space will be altered.

When Ryan first joined the Principals In Action Voxer group he remembers the discussion the group one day went towards a conversation around office space. Principals were bouncing different ideas back and forth with each other and then we talked about how it would be awesome to start videoing our office for some type of MTV Principal Cribs. What does your office look like? I am not only talking about your office, but the front office, and every office on your school site. Is it kid-centered? What type of art is on the wall? Is it welcoming? Is it professional looking?

When you walk into a school office, you should automatically smile. This is a place that should be welcoming and a place that everyone knows loves kids. Too often our offices are cramped, dim lite, not welcoming and have no pictures of kids. I aim to make our front office and my principal office a place where people know we are in the kid business and we love it. Ryan challenges everyone to look at your offices and make sure that they are kid-centered and create an environment that everyone knows that you love kids.

Challenge

Add something to your office that is welcoming and kid-friendly. Consider student seating, a bookcase with children's books, artwork, or activities to engage in with your students. Remember, an office doesn't have to be a place where students are sent for negative things. It can be a place for you to make positive connections.

Chapter 35

Being an Instructional Leader

(Mark French)

Some principals think being an instructional leader isn't possible with a focus on being a principal in action by being out of your office. Being out of your office is exactly where the instruction happens. Yes, it is important to set goals, review data, and complete teacher evaluations, but I have found that being a Principal In Action has enhanced my ability to be a better instructional leader.

By visiting classes, I can observe classroom climate and culture, see if expectations have been established and reinforced, and pay attention to instructional routines and transitions. By connecting with students during their learning, I can understand things from their perspective. Do they know the lesson objectives? Do they have a voice and choice in their learning? Do they get to use technology and other resources to demonstrate their knowledge? Are they engaged in learning activities with friends and classmates? Being a Principal In

Action gives me opportunities to observe instruction, pay attention to professional development needs, and see if teachers have the materials and resources they need.

One morning I was visiting classes during morning literacy time. I stopped in one third grade classroom and listened to the teacher introduce the story and literacy concepts for the week. In the next third grade classroom I visited, the teacher was discussing the same story and new vocabulary words. In the last third grade classroom I visited, the teacher was engaging students in comprehension questions from the same story. This demonstrated that teachers were planning together, following the recommended pacing of the literacy curriculum, and all third graders were being instructed in the same standards and objectives.

Jay has said this before, and he will say it again, a principal really can't know what's going on in the school if they spend the majority of time in their office. Jay takes pride in knowing what is happening in the school and visiting classrooms is really the only way he knows what is being learned as well as the planning that occurs among teachers to make sure that learning is occurring. Jay not only visits classrooms, he also attends planning meetings especially if a new curriculum is being introduced in the district. Listening to the teachers plan and work with their instructional coach has been eye opening for Jay. The depth of the conversations that he hears and is a part of not only around the content, but also the results of assessments and interventions that are in place. Implementing a new curriculum can be a daunting task and cannot be done from "the top down." Discussions about the successes and challenges are vital to the success of any curricular changes.

Jay has also been involved with a number of conversations with parents about instruction. Sometimes the parents are amazed that Jay really has an idea about what is happening in classrooms regarding instruction and curriculum. On more than one occasion a year, Jay will receive a phone call from a parent that has a message similar to this- "Do you have any idea what's happening in Mr./Mrs. (insert name here) classroom?" It can catch a parent off guard when Jay says, "I sure do. I was just in that class this morning and you'd be amazed at what they're learning!" Sometimes that diffuses the discussion while other times it becomes the basis for a really powerful discussion. If Jay wasn't in classrooms, attending curricular meetings, or having discussions with teachers, his effectiveness as an instructional leader would be greatly diminished.

Ryan also feels that being a connected educator has grown him as an instructional leader. Being an instructional leader is often looked at by overwhelmed leaders as impossible however we focus on what we feel is important. Without quality first instruction our students will not be accomplishing what we want to see happening in the classroom. Being a connected educator has allowed Ryan to visit many different schools and walk their classrooms. Walking their classrooms and conversing with many different principals and teachers allows Ryan to bring back many different ideas to his school and grows him as an instructional leader. Plant management tends to take up most of the time as a leader, but when we focus on our "why" we understand that instructional leadership is vitally important.

Challenge

Choose one curricular area to focus on. Spend time in those classrooms speaking with students and teachers to find out more about that curricular area. Do a little reading and research about that curricular area on your own to be able to add to the discussion with the teacher that will have an impact on the learning in those classrooms.

Chapter 36

Making Personal Connections with Students

(Jay Posick)

Principals need to get out of their office to get to know kids. They also need to connect with the teachers who work with those students as well as the students' families. I made a connection with a student that changed his perception of something that all of our schools have to do, fire drills. This student joined our school and I immediately made a connection with him. He struggled with everything about fire drills- not knowing when they would happen, how they were scheduled, how they actually happened, and the noise.

The story of this student came back to me at a PTO fundraiser. Our PTO is an amazing group of families that do so much for our school. The fundraiser was a Trivia Night and Mike Budisch, the Primary School principal, and I were put up for bid to be added to a table of parents and family members. Before the bidding started, one of the parents told a personal story about Mike and a personal story about me involving her family or her children. The story she told was about her son's fear of fire drills. I honestly didn't know that I had that much of an impact on her son or her family. The parent went on to tell those in attendance the fear her son had regarding fire drills. And then came the "mic drop moment". She told everyone about the one simple thing I did to help her son overcome his fear of fire drills. It wasn't anything mind-blowing at all. All I did was ask her son to run the fire drill with me. This 5th grader pulled the alarm, watched the students and staff leave the building, and reset the alarm, with a little help from the custodians and me. He still asked when the fire drills would be occurring, but he no longer had the fear surrounding everything else about the fire drills. Sometimes it's just the little things we do to connect with our students that make the biggest difference in their lives and in the lives of their families.

I also send videos to staff once in a while, often in our weekly staff nuts and bolts. A staff member wrote to me about a video I sent to the staff called "WE are here for YOU" from the Lakota School District. You can search for it on YouTube. We had a conversation over the span of a couple of emails about those students with whom we might not be as connected. I mentioned that I think it's important to change the students you connect with, and she agreed.

"I think it's good that your person can change and it's good that your assemblies are helping you grow relationships. You are making a difference every day. "

She then spoke about her son who is one of our students.

She said he used to say he wanted to be a lawyer but recently he has changed his mind. Now he wants to be a middle school teacher. I love it when our students realize that being an educator is what they want to do with their lives. Had the email stopped there, I would have been happy. But it didn't stop there. The staff member wrote this-

"Then most recently he told me that after he is a teacher, he wants to be a principal. Clearly....he can see that you love what you do.. "

What is the point of telling you this story? The point is, you never know when you are having an impact on someone. And if you don't know the impact you are having, make sure to make the impact a positive one.

Teamwork

Parent from Merton, WI

In 2015, our family moved into the Merton School District. At the time our boys were in seventh and fifth grade. We were looking for a fresh start for our fifth grader because he didn't have the greatest experiences at school prior to coming to Merton. For years we were working with a therapist, trying to get his ADHD under control, but nothing seemed to be working. Not until we met Mr. Posick.

Attending a new school was rough for Conor, but their bond started immediately. I think our bond with him did as well. That year Conor worked with multiple doctors trying to figure out the right combination of medication that would allow him to sit still and focus, but also to not lose his cool and become so frustrated. I can't tell you how many times we were called to come in and meet with Mr. Posick and Conor, not always because he was being consequenced, but to figure out how we could help Conor become as successful as we all knew he was capable of becoming.

The meeting that stands out the most was the day Conor was going to be removed from class because he still wasn't in a good place emotionally. He was going to start working one-on-one with a teacher, and not be in class with his peers because he often acted out. My husband and I were in tears because we didn't know what more we could do for Conor. Mr. Posick looked us both in the eye and said, "Don't worry. The way I see it, we're on plan B and there are twenty four more letters in the alphabet". It was then I knew Conor was in the best place he could be.

Today, you wouldn't recognize Conor as the same boy that first came to Merton. He is a happy, intelligent, athletic young man that is successful in so many ways. All the ways we knew he could be. My husband and I will forever be grateful to Mr. Posick for never giving up on Conor, and for being the rock this family needed him to be.

Ryan too believes strongly that relationships are the key. When you build strong relationships with students, it builds a foundation on which everything else can be built. When students have relationships with teachers at school they are more engaged and when students are more engaged, learning happens. Remembering back to teacher school, one of the things that were stressed was the fact that we shouldn't be sharing too much of our personal lives with our students, which I can agree with partly. There is no reason to share about a party that you attended, however, it is vital to make those personal connections with them and share things that happen in your life to build a strong relationship. Ryan decided that he wanted to be a transparent principal which allows his students, staff, and community to really get to know him. He shares often about what is going on in his life and connects those experiences back to relationships and conversations.

In Ryan's second year as being principal, he fell down the stairs at his house and broke his ankle in multiple places. He was rushed into emergency surgery and was out of work for sometime. Rather than coming up with some cool story, Ryan shared with everyone about his experience and allowed this to be a time for conversation and relationship building not a time for self-pity. To this day, Ryan still talks about this with students who ask or as a story of how if we get knocked down, we must get back up. Using things that happen in our lives connects students with us and builds those relationships that last a lifetime.

Mark believes making personal connections and developing relationships with students is one of the most important responsibilities as principal. This is not accomplished by being in your office. This is done by visiting classrooms and sitting down next to students. This is done by finding a student who deserves a positive phone call home. This is done by being on the playground, joining in games, and having conversations. This is done by attending out-of-school athletic or performing events. Sometimes this is done in a student's home.

When Mark started as principal in his current school, he joined a staff that had a practice of making home visits. One of the recommendations for teachers was to bring someone with them when making home visits. One first grade teacher's goal was to make a home visit for all of her students. Because she needed another colleague to join her, she asked Mark to go along on a number of those home visits. That was one of the most powerful things Mark has ever done as a principal. What an honor it is to be invited into someone's home. Mark has a special relationship two years later with the third graders whose home he was privileged to visit when they were in first grade.

Challenge

Think back to a student with whom you made a connection. If you are able, reach out to them or to their family to see how they're doing. If you cannot connect with them, think back on what you did to make that connection when they were in your school. Celebrate that connection and find another student to connect with this week.

OR

Try the 2x10 strategy with a student, spending 2 minutes with a student for 10 days in a row. Let the student lead the conversation. Show a real interest in them and what they are sharing with you. And once you have connected with that student, try it again with another student. Spending the time getting to know the student, with no strings attached, will certainly make their day.

Chapter 37

Building Relationships with Families

(Jay Posick)

One of the most important things to do as a principal is to build relationships. Some, including myself, would say relationships are the most important thing in a school. I really think the three "Rs" of education are relationships with students, relationships with staff, and relationships with families. If we don't have good relationships with our families, it's much more difficult to have good relationships with their children.

I have tried a number of ways to connect with families. I have occasional principal chats on specific topics. I use Instagram, Twitter, and Facebook to share the school's story. But my favorite way I connected with families was with a book discussion around *Beyond the Bake Sale* by Anne Henderson, Karen Mapp, Vivian Johnson, and Don Davies. I sent out an email to gather some interest and families signed on to read and discuss the book with me. Our district purchased the books for all interested and our book chat was underway. Parents joined me, and so did a couple of teachers.

Although the book helped us focus our conversations, it was the conversations themselves that helped our school become more family friendly. Ideas were shared that made communication better, and more two way. I really think that the word got around that I was a principal who is approachable, willing to learn, and will work together to help make sure that a student has a really good experience at our school. A principal's connection and relationships with families have a huge impact on the success of the students in a school.

Be Transparent With Your Families

Amber Teamann, Elementary Principal, Wylie, TX

Recognizing that by partnering with our families will allow us all to win for our students is the only impetus we need in order to make it happen!

Personally, I am a big fan of connecting with our families via social media. I want our families to see me as a wife, a mom, a leader who LOVES her job. I fully recognize that not all districts or organizations embrace that strategy, but using social media as a tool to connect with families as a CAMPUS is no longer an option we should ignore. We share so many glimpses into classrooms throughout the day via Facebook and Instagram and Twitter it would be hard pressed for a parent to make the claim that we aren't involved in instruction and believe in transparency between home and school. Adding our hashtag, #wearewhitt, to everything that we post allows families to see at a glance all of the great things we have going in our halls.

Another way I as the principal connect with families is by sending a postcard to each student each year. With over 650 Wolves, this is an ongoing challenge, but one that has made a HUGE difference in what we do at Whitt Elementary. Each week in our PLC I ask the teachers to give me one student that they would like to celebrate and to give me something specific to reference. I also give them their class lists where they check off the student each week. I write the postcard, and it typically looks like this, " Tenley, Mrs. Hunter tells me you've been working SO hard using your reading strategies.. and that you made a 100 this week on your reading test! Wow! She is proud of you and so am I!" The teacher gets a shout out, the parent gets something more than just " your kid is awesome" and we all win.

Greeting students, by name, each morning as they arrive was something that was important to my parents. I stand out, each day, from the time our doors open to when I go do announcements and make it my mission to be able to greet each family by name. My first year I studied our yearbook to help learn names faster. They say the most powerful word in the human language is your name, and I wanted our Wolves to be SEEN and know that who they were mattered to me. We also do our morning announcements on Facebook live. The parents are able to hear the exact same message their students hear. We announce upcoming events, the lunch menu and birthdays...all the things that matter!

Throughout the year, we highlight teachers and their contributions to all of our families. We want everyone to feel as they are a part of the Whitt family. We celebrate personal successes, professional leaps, and basically, all the things that matter to them. By doing this, we ensure that parents KNOW our staff...that they feel CONNECTED to our team...constant and regular communication allows everyone to feel like they are a part of the team... which is the relationship that we want!

Being a principal in the community that Ryan lives has helped build those relationships with the community. There is not a day that goes by that Ryan doesn't run into a student or family somewhere out in the community. This has allowed him to build relationships through conversation and sharing experiences. Many students from his school end up on sporting teams that he coaches, sitting behind him at church, or meeting him at the grocery store. If you look at these situations as a positive time to interact, it is an amazing opportunity to build relationships.

Mark shared in the previous chapter how powerful home visits are to making personal connections with students. It is also a powerful way to build relationships with families. During home visits, I watched teachers model asking questions of family members, engaging them in what they want for their child, and seeing how we can support them. In one home, we were greeted by the student, her siblings, her mother, and her grandmother. They prepared a Somalian feast for us and we got to converse and get to know them over a delicious meal. To this day, this family is one that Mark feels most connected to because of that home visit experience.

This past year, Matt Arend, a principal in Texas, shared on social media how he set up a desk in his school's lobby during conferences to greet, connect with, and assist families. Mark tried that during conferences in October and February. What a great way to connect and visit with families. Mark used to think about conference days as a time to be back in his office getting work done. Now, he looks at this opportunity to be out front welcoming, greeting, helping, and connecting with families.

Challenge

Think about the way you build relationships with the families at your school. Is there something you could change? Have you asked the families their opinion about the relationships they have with the school? Ask them and see what they have to say. Select one idea from this chapter, change it to meet your needs, and implement to improve the relationships you have with your school families.

Chapter 38

Say "Yes" To The Banana

(Ryan Sheehy)

The walk-a-thon is one of our biggest fundraisers every year. Every year, teachers compete to see how many laps they can get in and the kids create an energy that is contagious. Music is pumping, parents are cheering, and everyone is doing their best to complete as many laps as possible in the time allotted, all while raising money for the school.

As I do every year, I set a goal for myself. I was currently semi-training for a half marathon and my long run that week was supposed to be 8 miles. Instead of doing it that Saturday, I thought I would do it alongside the students. I was running strong with the first group of kids. At 1.5 miles, I continued my run into my office, while alrighty sweaty, changed into the Hawk mascot costume. Then I would head back outside to continue the walk-a-thon, this time wearing an extremely warm mascot costume. I ran for about another ½ mile and then retreated to my office to change once again. This routine would continue throughout the day.

When I was not running, I took the opportunity to talk and check in with parents. It is not often that as a principal, you get access to so many parents in such a positive situation. Parents were excited to see what their kids were doing and loved that our teachers were doing it alongside them. As I finished a conversation with one of the parents, I took off for another few laps. As I finished up those laps, a parent approached me as I was catching my breath. As I bent over breathing heavily, two kindergarten students came over and had a gift for me. They were holding a saran wrapped banana that was cut in half. They said, "Mr. Sheehy, we have something for you." At this point in the day, I had not drank enough water and definitely hadn't eaten anything. My stomach was not itself and the sight of the banana did not look appetizing. I quickly said thanks, but I am not hungry. The kids turned away and walked back towards their class and I continued to converse with the parent that I was talking with. I finished up the day and was sore for the majority of the weekend.

When Monday came around, the teacher of those two kids came in and asked if we could have a conversation. She wanted to tell me that those kids were so excited to give me the banana and when I said "no, thank you", their faces showed it all. This is a reminder that as an educator we hold so much power in a child's eyes. They look up to us and will do anything to make us happy. This reminded me that whenever kids come and offer you something, you stop, you give them your attention, you make a difference in a child's life.

Although Jay is a principal in an Intermediate School with students in 5th-8th grades, many of the students still celebrate their birthdays by bringing in birthday treats. Once in a while, there is even an extra treat for Jay to enjoy. Most often, Jay isn't in his office when the treat arrives. When that does happen, Jay goes on a search for the student to offer happy birthday wishes and to find out what the student will be doing for their birthday. It may not seem like a big deal, but it does make a difference.

Another thing Jay has begun is to write thank you notes to students and families that give him gifts before Winter Break or the end of the school year. It's important to Jay to recognize the efforts the students and families take when giving gifts. It takes only a couple of minutes for each note and a little bit of money for stamps, but the message that is sent in recognizing the gift is priceless. Jay does not send thank you notes in order to receive more gifts next year. He sends the notes because it's the right thing to do.

Mark's "Say 'Yes' to the Banana" story analogy has to do with putting yourself out there, even when you're tired or if it's not in your comfort zone. During a schoolwide fundraising assembly, Mark could see where things were headed when the assembly leaders were looking for a volunteer to do some crazy things. As they were talking about wanting the principal to come up front, Mark was secretly looking for the closest exit. As mentioned previously, Mark is an extroverted introvert and doesn't like being up in front of everyone doing silly things. I know, it seems incongruent with what a principal needs to do. Mark is willing to do crazy things, but he needs lead time to get mentally prepared. Being called on the spot up in front of an assembly is not generally in Mark's comfort zone. But, he knew that joining in, showing school spirit and doing something fun for the students was the right thing to do and it would have a positive impact. Mark stepped forward, put on the funny hat and glasses, danced around, and entertained the students.

Pay attention to your gut and your instincts. There are times when something was telling you to say "yes" to take that extra step, or to be present even if it meant you needed to do something you weren't totally comfortable with. Generally, your instincts are right so trust them.

Challenge

Visit a classroom today and make sure to spend just a couple of minutes talking with the first person who speaks to you. Don't worry about the topic. Just pay attention to them and give them a few minutes of your time that you might not have normally given. It will mean the world to them.

Chapter 39

#FeetUpFriday

(Mark French)

The **#FeetUpFriday** challenge was suggested by Jay in the Principals In Action Voxer group. Principals In Action maintain a positive attitude, promoting the great things happening in our schools and finding ways to reflect and acknowledge that. But sometimes we don't take the time to reflect on something great we did during the week, and the #FeetUpFriday challenge was meant to do just that.

Some Principals In Action have been accused of not addressing the problems, overlooking the challenges, and "sugar coating" things. I have certainly heard that in my administrative career. It's not that I want to ignore the negative things, it's just I want others to recognize there is more positive in our schools than negative. You do not ignore the work that needs to be done. You address that, but you also promote the positive things and accomplishments of others.

I have noticed it appears to be human nature to focus and perseverate on the negative, or perceived negative, comments. When meeting with teachers after a formative observation, I make sure to recap the one or two suggestions for improvement and the myriad of positive things. I want staff members to know there were so many great things I observed instead of focusing on the suggestions for improvement. I have to practice that myself. Even in my evaluations with my supervisors, I have to remember that suggestions and recommendations for improvement are an important part of reflecting, growing and getting better, but not the only thing. I reflect on the positive and the things that are going well to identify what occurred to make those happen.

Jay is much like me when it comes to dismissing the positive. It actually seems like many educators focus more on the negative than the positive- with their own evaluations, with conversations with supervisors, and with interactions with students and their families. That's unfortunate and something that needs to change. It's ironic that educators put a focus on the positives in student work while still providing feedback to improve. It's so important to stay as positive as possible as educators. There is enough negativity coming from outside education that we should support one another with as much positivity as we can, without the positivity being fake or unwarranted. The **#FeetUpFriday** challenge is one way to reflect on the week and celebrate something good that you did for your school, your family, or yourself during the week. There's nothing wrong with giving yourself a pat on the back.

The job of an educator is hard. The job of a leader is hard.

If we do not stop and focus on the things that are going well, burnout will occur sooner than we would ever expect. Ryan hears and sees the negative as well, but focuses on the positives while recognizing the things that aren't going as well. Keeping things fun and positive drastically impacts the culture in a school.

Challenge

Post a #FeetUpFriday message on Twitter, Instagram, Voxer or Facebook celebrating something awesome from the week. Encourage your staff to do the same thing and add your school hashtag.

Chapter 40

Unplugging, Disconnecting & Reflecting

(Mark French)

I'll let you in on a secret: it's okay to not always be a Principal In Action. I know, hard to believe, but we all need breaks, time away, and opportunities to unplug, disconnect, and reflect.

A happy, healthy principal makes for a happy, healthy school. ~ Mark French

When you are taking care of yourself, you will be in a better position to support your staff, students, and families. Some people unplug easier and better than others. Previous Principals In Action challenges have recommended removing notifications from your phone so you aren't drawn to or always tempted to check when you are with your family and away from work. Some principals have even deleted email apps from their phones so they are only checking messages at work. Principals, need to recharge their own batteries before recharging others. Don't neglect your interests, hobbies, and passions. I know a number of Principals In Action who are runners and nothing stops them from engaging in this activity. I'm impressed by the daily running streaks some members of my PLN have attained. They don't let anything get in their way be it weather, schedules, and family commitments.

Jay is one of those running principals I mentioned. What started as a personal challenge to get in better shape in 1987 became a way for Jay to have uninterrupted time away from social media, text messages, and school email. The reason for Jay's running craze started when he was coaching high school boys volleyball. Jay prided himself on being in shape and it became a competition with the boys he was coaching. When Jay realized he couldn't keep up, he was determined to get into better shape and started running. That first run was in August of 1987 and he hasn't missed a day since. His streak is now over 11,500 days. These daily runs are just the thing that Jay needs every day to unplug, disconnect, and reflect. Jay doesn't run with his phone so the distraction of notifications isn't there. Jay's daily run is a time to reflect on the day to come or the events of the day, and sometimes the best ideas come while he is out for a run.

Jay has also developed a habit that helps to keep him disconnected at night. His computer is closed and his phone is put on silent at 9:00 every school night. Jay has often said to his PLN that nothing good ever happens on school email after 9:00. That's reason enough not to check your school email before going to bed. We have all read that one last email that clutters your mind and hinders your sleep. Jay has found this one little rule has made for better sleep. And guess what? That email you didn't read at 9:00 will still be there in the morning waiting for you.

Unplugging and disconnecting are two very hard things for Ryan to do. He struggles with turning his phone or computer off and allowing time for other things. Without doing those two things, he does allow time to reflect and has found it to help him grow exponentially. Balance has been something that we have talked about many times in the voxer group and different members have even written a book about it. Ryan has been able to turn email off on his phone on the weekends and this has allowed him to engage with his family in a more intentional way.

Challenge

Recommit to engaging in one of your passions, don't neglect yourself. Do you need to commit to a daily walk or workout? Do you need to get back into the kitchen cooking or baking? Do you need to carve out time for pleasure reading? Do you need to restart your creative juices by singing, painting or making music? Better yet, do you have a family member or friend who will join you in your passion to hold you accountable?

Chapter 41

Engaging In Your Own Learning

(Mark French)

Principals In Action never stop learning. They're always reflecting, gathering data, asking for feedback, and working to be better. You are responsible for your own professional growth and development and there are so many options for you to choose from. Attending national conferences and connecting with others in person can be a great opportunity for some. But, even if you have limited professional development resources there are low or no-cost learning opportunities through social media.

I engage in my own learning in a variety of ways. A number of years ago I started attending EdCamps at the encouragement of other educators I met on Twitter. It's a special moment to meet someone in person with whom you have connected through Twitter or Voxer. You already have an instant connection and there are so many great educators to learn with and from at EdCamps. Connecting in person with other educators who have inspired, motivated, and supported me has been priceless professional development. I visited Jon Harper in Maryland, Andy Jacks and Justin Birckbichler in Virginia, Jay Posick in Wisconsin, Jonathon Wennstrom and Julie Mytych in Michigan, Joe Mullikin in Illinois, and a whole big group of Principals In Action at the National Principal Conferences in Philadelphia in July 2017 and in Spokane in July 2019. I have visited principal colleagues locally, across Minnesota, and around the country. These visits always are inspiring and help me continue my learning. Being actively engaged with Twitter and Voxer allows me to connect with and learn from others. I have participated in and led Twitter chats that bring people together around a common theme. I listen to podcasts, read blogs, and participate in webinars and enjoy these platforms because they allow me to access learning on my schedule, whenever I want.

Jay loves finding ways to learn that are a bit out of the ordinary. Attending conferences, mostly in Wisconsin where he lives, allows Jay to learn with principals and other educators who have great ideas to share, a great message, and a push to try something new that will benefit the school community. In Jay's opinion, the best learning doesn't necessarily happen during the sessions. It happens in those moments before, between, or after sessions. Jay also likes to sit with people that he doesn't really know and engage in conversations, especially when the presenters allow for reflection and conversation.

Jay's favorite learning opportunities are EdCamps, the "unconference" which allows attendees to select what they want to learn about and also proposing sessions to facilitate or lead. EdCamps happen all over the country at all times of the year. Some districts even use EdCamps for their professional development days. The only real issue Jay has with EdCamps is the lack of attendance by administrators, both at the building level and the district level. If you haven't attended an EdCamp, Jay encourages you to find one in your area, attend, and learn with the teachers. The biggest consideration to keep in mind is that you don't want to come back from an EdCamp or conference with so many ideas and changes that it makes the teachers' heads spin. Get together with some of the teachers and share your ideas, working together to find those things that could benefit the students and the staff.

Ryan had been on Facebook for years, but Twitter for only a few. In the beginning, he was apprehensive, he didn't know what to expect. He thought that it would take away from my family time and other duties. The most important thing is that he kept an open mind. He now says that being connected on Twitter has revived his passion for education and allowed him to grow in so many ways. Twitter allows professional development in your pajamas, why not take advantage of that.

One day at a district meeting, Ryan overheard a table saying "I bet he is twittering". It caught his attention. He approached the table and he mentioned that he wasn't on Twitter, but he does use it and he absolutely loves it. That began a conversation on having an open mind. That is all he asks. Try something new today and expand your toolbox.

Always Learning

Greg Moffitt, Elementary Principal, Winters, CA

Being one of the Principals In Action is being a principal that is always learning. For me, that learning accelerated the minute I started using social media to reach out and get connected with other educators – educators who are doing great things to make their schools better for students and staff.

The work we do in education is far too difficult and far too important to do alone. And if we're trying to do it on our own, we're probably doing it wrong. The job of being a principal can be lonely, but it doesn't have to be that way. There is an entire world of educational leaders waiting to help and share ideas. It is our job, as educators, to seek out those ideas and to make them our own.

I signed up for Twitter in the summer of 2014, but until this past summer, I think I had posted four times. Maybe. And I only joined because I was at a workshop where Eric Sheninger (@E_Sheninger) literally stopped his presentation and told us all to do so. So I did. And then I never used it. Fast forward to March 2018 when I went to a conference where George Couros (@gcouros) was presenting. He said to use Twitter to "make the positives so loud that the negative becomes almost impossible to hear." I posted a few more times and then I still didn't do anything with Twitter. What can I say, I'm slow to warm. To be honest, I'm not really sure why it took so long for me to use Twitter. Maybe I was worried about putting my thoughts out there? Maybe I didn't think I had anything to offer? Maybe I was worried about what other people would say?

Well, that's the point. The point is to see what people say: to get new ideas, to share ideas, and to be challenged! Because once I jumped in and got connected, I became a better principal. And more importantly, our school got better, too. It is because of Twitter that I was introduced to Mark French (@PrincipalFrench) and the #GoodNewsCalloftheDay. It has transformed the culture of our school and my relationships with students and their families. It has transformed me. It is because of Twitter that I was introduced to Sean Gallard (@smgaillard) and the challenge to #CelebrateMonday which has transformed my mindset and outlook.

It is because of Twitter that I was encouraged to read #CultureMatters and was inspired by Jay Billy (@JayBilly2) to rediscover my passion and my joy. It has transformed who I am as a principal. It is because of Twitter that I saw Jeff Kubiak (@jeffreykubiak) reading bedtime stories and Mandy Ellis (@mandyeellis) inviting her students to have popsicles with the principal. You don't need to be on Twitter or Facebook or Instagram to be a #PrincipalInAction, but you do need to connect. You need to reach out to other principals. You need to constantly seek out new ideas and make them work for your school, with your students, and the staff you work with, too.

As principals, one of the most important actions we can take is to passionately model what it means to be a lifelong and connected learner, because a Principals In Action, is a principal that is always learning.

Challenge

Find an EdCamp in your area and attend. Invite your principal friends, or your superintendent, to join you and learn right along with the teachers. If EdCamps aren't your thing, attend a state or national conference and sit with someone you don't know, introduce yourself, and learn right along with them.

Chapter 42

Mobile Offices

(Mark French)

Because Principals In Action focus on being out of their office, they need ways to continue their work and to communicate with others when they are out and about. Some principals use furniture, equipment, tools and resources that allow them to continue their work when they are out of their office. Some PIAs (Principals In Action) have embraced the concept of mobile offices to help them connect, be visible, and be productive.

I have yet to utilize a physical mobile office like others have. I have found that my smartphone works well as my mobile office. I can stay connected with the office staff via email and text messages. I use my phone's camera to capture great things happening around school and share that to social media. I use apps like ColorNote and Evernote to make lists and keep track of things and I use Google Docs, Sheets and Slides for other work projects.

Some PIAs have repurposed media carts that support their laptops, coffee mugs, and other supplies. Some have purchased mobile stands that serve as their office on wheels. Do a Google search and a myriad of mobile desk options with a range of price points will pop up. Some principals use a fanny pack or backpack that they fill with what they need. Those with physical mobile desks have personalized them and made them colorful, fun and interesting.

Jay has a mobile office that consists of his cell phone, Chromebook, and padfolio. The staff knows how to get in touch with Jay and most rarely call his office. If staff need to find Jay they either text him, send him a direct message on Twitter, send him an email, or send him a message through Google hangouts. In emergencies, staff might call his cell phone. Regardless, staff know if they reach out Jay will be there as quickly as possible. If a family comes into the office, Jay's secretary is able to quickly text him and he comes to the office right away. The key to being a principal in action out of your office is to still be able to be available. If your staff knows about the ways to get in touch with you, there really isn't a need to be in your office very much at all.

Ryan has a mobile office that he carries in the palm of his hand. We are at a time in society where cell phones have become so versatile that they are mini-computers. There is no need to lug other things around and there is no need to be tethered by wires. The way Ryan's campus is doesn't lend itself to a mobile office cart or other mobile office contraptions, but he does have spaces around campus that if he needs to meet with someone or take a call he can pop into.

Challenge

Find something that can serve as your mobile office. It can be your smartphone, a fanny pack, a backpack, or a mobile desk. Be sure to inform your office staff on how you can be reached (walkie-talkie with/without an earpiece, phone call, text message, email message) and let your staff know that you are using your mobile office to be visible and to engage and observe teaching and learning.

ABOUT THE AUTHORS

 Jay has been an educator for over 30 years with 29 of those years spent at the middle school level as either a teacher or school level administrator. Jay believes all students and the teachers and support staff that serve them deserve his best everyday. He is collaborative leaders working together to make sure that students have the best learning environment possible with engaging lessons and learning activities, and choice to express how and what they learn.

Jay is married to his beautiful wife and has a daughter who attends UW-Oshkosh where she is studying education. Jay enjoys running, playing poor golf with my daughter, watching my daughter dance, fishing, and spending uninterrupted time with family. Being a connected educator is important to Jay and he is active on social media (@posickj and @mertonint on Twitter and our school's Facebook and Instagram pages) to share the great things his students and staff do every day.

Ryan was raised in Southern California where his diverse education experiences all started. He attended public school, private school, and was homeschooled. He has seen and been part of all types of education systems, which gives him a different perspective. Ryan is a passionate educator that has made it his mission to help everyone live up to their potential and unleash their power to change the life of a child.

He also has an immense dedication for kids and for making sure all educators understand the power they have in a child's life. Ryan was a physical education teacher for ten years before taking the leap from teacher to administrator. After serving two years as a high school vice-principal, Ryan is now the lead learner/principal of an elementary school in Concord, California. Ryan prides himself as being someone who can build strong school culture and that is exactly what has happened at the schools where he has worked.

Ryan works in the community where he lives, which allows him to build many relationships that foster a great learning environment for staff, students and families. Ryan also travels and speaks about creative educational practices and how we all have the power to Be the One for Kids. Ryan is the author of Be The One For Kids. The book was written to help every educator unleash their power to change the life of a child.

Ryan's wife, Barbara, and four children, Robert, Joshua, Julianna, and Zachary, are the light of his world. Ryan and his family reside in Concord, California.

Mark is a thirty-eight year veteran educator serving his 23rd year as a principal. He has worked in urban and suburban, public and private, and elementary and middle school settings.

Mark has been blessed with a career that has allowed him to learn from students, parents, family members, teachers, colleagues, friends, and so many who have taught, mentored, influenced, and made him reflective and better. One of Mark's proudest honors was being named Minnesota's 2015 National Distinguished Principal.

MORE FROM EDUGLADIATORS

Available everywhere books are sold.

The Teacher & The Admin
By Kris Kris Felicello (@KFelicello) & Gary Armida (@GaryArmida)

Today's kids are simply amazing. They are succeeding despite a myriad of challenges faced every day. Schools are racing to not only meet their needs, but to evolve to give kids what they truly deserve: a more meaningful education. The only way the education system can transform is to work together. The only way the education system can transform is to work together. Teachers and Administrators must work in a partnership to make lasting changes to a system that has historically been slow to evolve. The Teacher (Gary Armida) and the Admin (Dr. Kris Felicello) give the blueprint to this partnership to make schools better for kids.

My Pencil Made Me Do It: A Guide to Sketchnoting
By Carrie Baughcum (@HeckAwesome)

The pencil is a single tool that has the power to reset mindsets, enhance thinking, improve retention, recall, and comprehension, calm us and make us smile…all this from a pencil. My Pencil Made Me Do It is a unique, hands-on, create-to-connect and doodle-to-learn book that will have readers discovering powerful moments, learning the power behind visual thinking, and doodling to learn. Through honest perspective and creative insight, Carrie opens educators and students to visualize their thinking and their learning. While enabling them to experience how they can bring visual thinking into our world.

Champ For Kids
by Kelly Hoggard (@champforkids)

This book is for every teacher, no matter their level of experience. For seasoned veterans confidently navigating around the ring, find inspiration to continue to push on into the next round. For educators that feel as though every time they get on their feet, they are bruised and battered by another jab, make connections to this book to help develop a solid foundation towards becoming a champion. Finally to preservice educators standing outside the ring unsure if they have what it takes when the day comes to be tagged in, find the guidance and essentials needed to head into the ring. Champ For Kids inspires advocacy, going to the ropes for students, coaching them through mistakes so they land the TKO!

Bold Humility: Growing Students by Empowering Teachers
By David M. Schmittou (@daveschmittou)

It may seem like an oxymoron, but it is anything but that. BOLD humility is that secret "it" factor that we look for when trying to discover greatness. It is the balance of confidence and grace. It is wisdom coupled with vulnerability. It is the ability to bravely embrace what you know while being willing to seek support where you need it the most. In this book, Dave takes a look at how educators can embrace BOLD humility to help tap into the greatness inside all of us. By sharing his own struggles coupled with his own successes, Dave paves a path that allows us all to walk away feeling empowered and ready to tackle the challenges that await us all.

The Future Is Now: Looking Back to Move Ahead

By Rachelle Dene Poth (@Rdene915)

If we are dedicated to facilitating the best futures for
our students, we must be fully invested in lifelong
learning and our personal and professional growth.
In this book, the reader will hear from different
educators, each sharing anecdotes and wisdom
about becoming more connected, taking risks, and
using failures and past experiences to help prepare
for the future. Inspirational quotes appear throughout, prompting introspection and a call to action.
A student also lends her perspective in a chapter,
offering reflection from the other side of the classroom. When we strengthen ourselves as educators,
we in turn empower others to do the same. Stronger
together, we face whatever the future of learning
will bring.

R.E.S.U.L.T.S.: Promoting Positive Behavior and Responsibility for Learning

by Krista Venza (@kristavenza) & Jon Treese (@jt2510)

R.E.S.U.L.T.S. is a book that provides applicable
strategies for teaching students to make positive
choices, take necessary action and promote growth.
This book is an enjoyable mixture of inspiring stories
and a framework that promotes positive behavior
and responsibility for learning. From R.E.S.U.L.T.S.,
educators will feel empowered to make a difference in
the lives of their students.

Made in the
USA
Lexington, KY

55881784R00146